Other People's Children:

My Life and Family

Mavis Humby
Plaisted Publishing House, Ltd
New Zealand

Copyright Mavis Humby 2018

Dedication

This book is dedicated to my wonderful husband Patrick, for all the happy memories he's given me. He has sat beside me as I wrote this memoir, remembering long forgotten details when my memory failed me.

Also, to Lisa and Nicholas, who shared their lives with the many children we have cared for over the years, and Karen my niece, whose help was invaluable in bringing this book to print.

And lastly to my lovely friends, who encouraged me to write this book after my relating funny stories at our monthly gatherings over the last forty years: Mary R., Kath, Margaret, Ceinwen, Sheila, Jackie, and not forgetting Val and Mary G, who are sadly no longer with us.

Thank you all from the bottom of my heart.

Contents

Where it all Started

Forty years down the line, I still ponder and think to myself, 'How did it all begin?'

It all began in Aberystwyth, in Mid-Wales where my parents met for the first time whilst on holiday with their friends. My mother, who was from Manchester, was with Florence Keene and my father, from Llanymynech, with his friend, Wynne Jones. They all met up on the promenade.

Dad was a reporter in Shropshire and Mum worked in a bank in Manchester. The couple's love flourished, and they were married in 1933. A newspaper clipping from 1933 captured the happy couple.

Marriage notice... *The marriage took place at the Church of the Holy Innocents, Fallowfield, Manchester, on Thursday 1st June 1933, of Miss Winifred Stott, daughter of Mr. and Mrs. F. H. Stott, of Burnage, and Mr. Edward Parry Jones, a member of the editorial staff of the Cheshire Observer. The bride was formerly on the staff of Messrs Lewis's Bank, Manchester, and her father is well known on the Manchester Stock Exchange. The bridegroom's home was at Llanymynech, near Oswestry.*

The ceremony was conducted by the Rev. Samuel Taylor (rector), and the service was choral, Dr. Kingsley being at the organ. The bride, who was given away by her father, wore a dress of ivory charmeuse satin with wreath and veil and carried a bouquet of red roses. The bridesmaids were Miss Barbara Stott (sister of the bride) and Miss Florence

Keen. They were dressed in floral georgette gowns with picture hats and carried bouquets of carnations and Lily of the Valley. Mr. Ewart Sampson, of Llanymynech, was best man, and Mr. Glyn Richards of Shrewsbury, (a cousin of the bridegroom,) was groomsman.

A reception was held at Messrs Duncan and Foster's Café, Oxford Road, Manchester, and the honeymoon is being spent in the Isle of Man.

On the 24th October 1935, the couple had their first child-my sister Kathleen. Two years later, Mum suffered a miscarriage. In November 1940, I was born at Stanley Nursing Home in Chester. It was the night the only bomb fell on the city, and the doctor said to Mum, "Thank you for waiting until after the bomb fell before calling me out."

Their third child, David, was born on 11th September 1943. Being the only boy, he was spoilt by our Mum and Kathleen. I always thought he received better treatment than us girls, as his gifts were always larger.

More about my mother...
Mum was a very good athlete in her younger days, and I still have one of the medals she won for running.

She was, bless her, very loving, but suffered from bad moods- usually on a Sunday when we were all at home.

She would rant and rave and would often say, "I wouldn't give tuppence for the lot of you."

Dad would stick his head in the newspaper and we'd try to keep out of her way until she calmed down.

She frequently compared us to her friend's children who, according to her, were angels. I once accidentally knocked the clock off the mantelpiece, and she slapped me across the face. I ran out of the house intending to run away but wasn't brave enough, and returned when she had calmed down.

My sister always said I was a battered child, and Mum would slap my legs while I escaped up the stairs after being told off, although I don't remember that. Thinking back, these moods were the beginning of her dementia, which wasn't diagnosed until she was in her seventies.

Dad would do anything for a peaceful life and never retaliated. Mum was extremely jealous and regularly accused him of looking at other women. I suspect something occurred early on in their marriage, which sparked her suspicion long before I was born. None of us realised at the time that she was suffering from some sort of illness.

Mum was always busy as she was in numerous voluntary organisations. In Newtown, for many years she sold National Savings stamps and would sit in a room in town on a certain day each week while people called to buy them. She loved publicity and having her photograph taken. If a photographer was around, she would always make sure she was in the front row.

More about my father... As a young lad, Dad lived with his maiden Aunt Margaret in the village of Llanymynech, a small Welsh border village. Aunt Margaret was a dear lady who regularly went to church in the village. Dad lived with her because his own mother had found herself pregnant and unmarried, which was a scandal in those days.

He attended church every Sunday, a habit that stayed with him for the rest of his life.

He did well at school and was one of the first pupils to attend Carreghofa School in the village when it was first built. It is said that he read every book in the library.

My memory of my dad is how he always wore a suit and tie with black shoes, never brown, even on the beach. The only change in his clothes during summer was a thinner jacket. Dad never dressed casually and at the end of the day would say, "Does anyone mind if I take my tie off?"

I don't think Dad knew how to give physical affection as he hadn't experienced much tenderness in his childhood. He did care for us and hardly ever shouted—well only occasionally, such as when we fought in the back of the car and he'd have to pull over and stop. He never did any domestic chores around the house, Mum did everything. She was even in charge of the finances. I never saw Dad clear the table or wash up. He always had his face in a newspaper and read several every day. He loved watching television, particularly entertainment shows. He was extremely knowledgeable about current affairs and gave talks on this subject. His one and only hobby was playing bowls, which he played regularly at the Oswestry Wynnstay Bowling Club. For a time he was president, and my brother David has since followed in his footsteps. Fifty years later, David is still president of the same club.

Dad suffered from angina for many years, and after walking a short distance he would have to stop till the pain in his shoulder stopped. If it didn't then he would take a tablet. I was always conscious of this and frightened he would collapse and die, but he lived until he was eighty-three.

My parent's first home was a semi-detached house in Green Lane, Vicars Cross, Chester where Dad was a reporter for the Liverpool Daily Post.

In 1983, Mum and Dad celebrated their Golden Wedding Anniversary. It was exciting to see this article in the local newspaper:

The Golden Wedding Couple

They are Mr. Ted Parry Jones, a Llanymynech man who served his apprenticeship in journalism on the Advertizer just after the First World War and subsequently returned to become an editor, and his wife, Winifred, who live on Balmoral Crescent in Oswestry.

Mr. and Mrs. Parry Jones were married at Holy Innocents Parish Church, in Manchester. Mr. Frederick Hastings Stott—her father, worked at the Manchester Stock Exchange for 45 years.

For over 20 years, Mr. and Mrs. Parry Jones made their home in Chester, where Mr. Parry Jones, after spells on the Shrewsbury Chronicle and Newport & Market Drayton Advertiser, was initially on the Cheshire Observer and then was for many years with the Liverpool Daily Post & Echo.

In 1950, he became editor of the Montgomeryshire Express and the Radnor Times, moving to Oswestry in 1955 to become editor of the Advertizer. For several years, he was also the editor of the old Saturday Express, which was published at weekends.

Here is another excerpt from a local paper:

He [Mr. Parry Jones] retired in 1969 but has done considerable part-time journalistic work for national and weekly newspapers.

Mr. Parry Jones is a life member of the Newspapers Press Fund and a former member of the Chester and North Wales Committee of the Fund. He was recently made a life member of the National Union of Journalists which he joined in 1924.

Mr. Parry Jones is a former president of Oswestry Rotary Club and of Oswestry Probus Club. Mrs. Parry Jones is a former president and secretary of Oswestry Inner Wheel Club. She has also been a member of Croesoswallt Townswomen's Guild for over 25 years, during which time she has been president, secretary and treasurer.

Mr. and Mrs. Parry Jones both served on the local Committee of the Shropshire Voluntary Helping Hand Association.

For many years, Mr. Parry Jones was Press Officer to the Orthopaedic Hospital and still serves in the same capacity for the League of Friends.

His wife is a member of the League's Voluntary Services Committee. Mr. Parry Jones is a member of the executive committee of the Oswestry Council of Churches.

Mr. and Mrs. Parry Jones have been active members of the Presbyterian Church of Wales in Chester, Newtown and Oswestry and Mr. Parry Jones was elected as an elder of City Road, Chester, The Crescent Church Newtown, and Oswald Road Church, Oswestry where he was Church Secretary. Mr. and Mrs. Parry Jones were lifelong Liberals. They had three married children, Mrs. Kathleen Parry, Summerseat, nr Bury, Mrs. Mavis Humby, Middleton Road, Oswestry and Mr. David Parry-Jones, Assistant Editor of the Chester Chronicle.

There was a family celebration at the home of their son, David, in Higher Kinnerton, near Chester on Saturday night.

Homes

We first lived at Green Lane, Vicars Cross in Chester. Our house had a small back garden and a garage.

One of my earliest memories is of sitting at the end of David's pram and going into the little post office at the end of the road realising I could just reach over the counter. I was probably three or four years old.

I was a painfully shy child, although my friends now find this hard to believe. Mum would be annoyed when anyone spoke to me as I would hide behind her back.

Once my sister borrowed someone's horse, which she kept in an orchard not far away but, unfortunately, whilst stroking it one of her friends was badly bitten, so the horse had to be returned. Another thing I remember is Kathleen keeping pet mice in a cage in our little outhouse. One day my friend visited, saw the mice, and ran right home screaming.

Kathleen organised concerts for family and neighbours and we would sell tickets. The concerts were held in our garage. My speciality act was singing Bobby Shafto. I can still remember the words.

Being shy, I hated performing in public, and especially dreaded Sunday school anniversaries held annually at our church in City Road, Chester.

11

Each Sunday morning we had to recite a verse from the bible at the front of the church. I can still remember those verses. Sometimes I hadn't learnt one and so I would stand up and say, "God is Love" or "Jesus Loves Me," as these were the shortest ones I could remember.

As we entered the church every Sunday morning a kind man would give us a barley sugar sweet. (Coincidentally, many years later, my brother David worked with him at The Chester Chronicle where he was sub-editor.) We found the service boring and often giggled and misbehaved. Kathleen would whisper something in my ear like, "Mrs. Dog Dirt." This would set me off laughing and Dad would scowl at us. On the way home from church we called at the sweet shop for a treat, but we were told not to eat them until after our dinner.

It was very tempting to just try one- and this habit has stayed with me. I do enjoy a few sweets or chocolate in the evening. Dad always had sweets and I often pinched one or two.

Sunday afternoons usually found our family going for a walk. The Groves by the River Dee in Chester was our favourite place and one year I remember it froze and people walked on it.

One of my favourite games while we were walking was pretending Mum and Dad were my horses and I'd herd them with my stick. Dad was called Blackie and Mum, Prince. How I loved this make-believe game!

I clearly remember my first day at infant school. No nursery school for us, as we went straight into education. The school was Cherry Grove Infant School in Chester and, being shy, I hated going in that first day. I cried when Mum left. Another little girl assured me she would soon be back to collect me.

I was good at sulking. At my birthday parties I was never allowed to have the prize if I won a game. Mum said, "It's your party, so you can't have the prize." I thought it was most unfair! Sulking never seemed to change the outcome though.

I don't remember having large presents for birthdays or Christmas but, one year, I remember seeing a toy sewing machine in a shop window. I begged to have this sewing machine. This time I didn't have to sulk as come Christmas morning, there it was. However, I was never very good at sewing, although I did manage to pass my O level GCE needlework exam. I didn't understand what I was making when I read the brief, yet managed to somehow pass. I started following the instructions and when I looked over at what other girls were doing, I realised I was making a gusset for a pair of knickers! I had to make a dress, but wouldn't have been seen dead in it.

I didn't enjoy school much and spent most of my time chatting. I failed cookery, even though I was good at it, but I'm sure it was because my fishcakes fell apart. Once I was sent to the Headmistress' office to be reprimanded. I regret now not listening more. Dad taught me how to swim and would hold his hand under my chin, then let go so I would sink. To this day I don't like having my head underwater! I didn't learn to swim properly until visiting Grandma Kynaston's house in Oswestry where the local baths were just down the road.

Being the middle child, I always felt I didn't get treated as well as Kathleen and David. Kathleen was the eldest, David the youngest and the only boy, but I was just in the middle.

When I was nine years old, Dad accepted the position of Editor of the Montgomeryshire Express, so we all moved to live in Newtown. My parents bought a detached house on Canal Road set high up on a hillside. It was called Nantgwyllt.

There were raspberry bushes and asparagus in the large back garden and a portico stood on the left-hand side. There was a reception room on either side with the kitchen at the back. Three bedrooms and a bathroom were upstairs. A Corona Gem solid fuel fire stood in the kitchen and burned smokeless fuel and it also heated our water.

Not far away was the canal where some gypsies parked. Mum befriended them and sometimes the children came to our house for a bath. I still have a fondness for the traditional gypsy way of life.

Every evening was spent playing with my friend Susan Davies, and sometimes I would sleep at her house. It was called Kymrick House and I was terrified of her dad as he would shout at us for talking in bed.

My favourite game was playing fairs where I attached trailers at the back of the buckboard (a kind of go-cart) and rode around the house pretending we were moving to another town. I think for this reason I loved touring in our caravan.

Once I was asked to present a bouquet to an important lady and wore a smart dress. I have a photograph of the occasion, but wish I could remember who she was. Pictured below is the event.

While living at Nantgwyllt, my Aunty Barbara, who was my Mum's youngest sister, died. She committed suicide after marrying a really rotten character. He didn't treat her well and managed to sell her mother's house from under her nose. I am not sure how he managed it, but the result was poor Grandma Stott had to live in a caravan on a farm site in Cheshire.

Aunty Barbara had one daughter, Gillian, who was nine when her mother died. She went to stay with Mum's older sister Aunty Kath and her husband, Uncle Clarry. He was a chartered accountant and they were quite well-off. Aunty Kath had one son, Paul, but unfortunately lost their daughter, Anne, when she was five years old due to an asthma attack. However, some weeks after Gillian moved in with them, Aunty Kath was on the phone begging Mum to raise Gillian. Mum had no choice but to agree.

Gillian was sixteen months younger than me, and I was very jealous of her. I recall how we had two female rabbits and each had a litter of young. Gillian swapped over the babies, which resulted in the baby rabbits being killed by the mums.

She was not a nice child and Aunty Kath paid for her to go to private school. Gillian and I occasionally visited Aunty Kath and Uncle Clarry and would go to the shops where Gillian would be treated to presents. Aunty Kath would say to me, "You don't mind do you? She hasn't got a mother." I did mind and attending private school didn't make Gillian a nicer child.

I often suffered a pain in my stomach and it usually subsided after a while, but I never told anyone as I was scared I would have to go into hospital. It was only at the age of fifteen when I had to tell Mum. I was taken to the RSI Hospital in Shrewsbury, but after being admitted the pain went away. However, it was decided it best to remove my appendix.

After the operation, a lady at the end of the ward suffered bad wind and was trumping and belching all night. I hid under the bedclothes as I suffered a fit of the giggles.

On my discharge home Grandma Stott, who had been staying at our house, passed away. When the undertakers came to carry her body down the stairs, Mum told them to mind her head as they were quite rough with her. It was a rather bleak homecoming for me from the hospital.

Mum was a big supporter of Dr. Barnardo, who in 1867 organised a charity for children. When we lived in Oswestry she distributed savings boxes that were in the shape of a house. All money raised supported his children's homes. Pictured is a photograph of my mother opening Dr. Barnardo boxes.

Once a year she organised a party for all the children who had boxes. They'd bring them along and as they enjoyed the food, drink and games, the money boxes would be emptied and counted. She really loved these parties.

Mum was a smart dresser, and I never saw her wearing trousers. She especially loved hats and every Sunday she attended church wearing a hat. If my father asked her what anything had cost, Mum always told him an amount less than what she had spent. Mum was in charge of all money matters and entered every expenditure carefully into a book. I do the same now. However, Dad's wages were not large, and she occasionally would have to make an appointment with the bank manager to ask for help. They tended to live beyond their means with Mum always believing things would improve the following month. My parents lived on one wage as Mum never earned after they married.

Mum didn't enjoy housework or cooking, although she did make a nice Madeira cake. Often when we returned from school we would find Mum out somewhere and on her return, she would say, "Oh, what can we have for tea?"

Mum and Dad always ate dinner at dinner time and tea at tea time. We always sat at the table never eating on our laps. They enjoyed tripe and brains, which was a popular dish in those days. For supper, sometimes they would have a bowl of bread and milk, or when in season, a plate of peas fresh out of the pod with butter.

My parents did tend to argue a lot and sometimes would go for days without speaking, but they couldn't live without each other.

One person I couldn't live without was my best friend, Doreen. She was my best friend while we lived in Newtown, and we met while in a class at Newtown Girls High School. Doreen and I always said we would keep in touch, and sixty years later we still speak on the phone. Kathleen went out with Doreen's brother, Bobby, for many years but the romance ended. He later became editor of the Shropshire Star.

Holidays

Every year our family would go away on our summer holidays. During the year we were made to save up each week and Mum divided the amount. Each morning we received a packet containing our daily spends. This meant we could buy sweets, ice cream, visit the fair or, best of all, go roller-skating. I loved skating around the rink to music, and it was probably my favourite thing to do on holiday.

We made a really early start to travel the long distance to the South coast where we often spent our holiday. The first thing I did when arriving at the beach was to strip off and put my bathing costume on as I couldn't wait to run into the sea.

Sometimes it would be a flat in Rhyl where I would spend most of the holiday leading the donkeys on the beach while giving children rides.

We mostly stayed in self-catering apartments but occasionally, in a  boarding house. At one of these, I can remember every morning a man would say, "Morning all." We began to anticipate when he was going to say it and had a fit of giggles as he approached. I'm sure he thought we were mad by the end of the week!

Sometimes we travelled to the south coast, mostly to Southsea or Worthing, where the sun always seemed to shine. Kathleen would take me as an alibi when she met a boy who worked in the local camera shop.

She was slim, pretty, and attractive to boys. When we returned I never divulged where we had been or who we had met. What a good little sister I was!

On one trip I saw a Labrador puppy with two others in a pet shop window. I asked if I could have one and on being told no, immediately stopped speaking to everyone. I probably ruined the whole holiday for me and everyone else. I just didn't speak to them for the whole two weeks. I thought my parents would give in and let me have the puppy, but they never did and we returned home without one.

One very wet holiday in Aberystwyth in 1951, we went to see The Tale of Hoffman starring Moira Shearer about a poet and the three women he loved. We saw that film three times just to escape the rain. We really hated the story by the end of the week!

I also recall the moments the sun shone on the beach, and how we spread out all our belongings and settled down, only for Mum to decide there was a much nicer spot a little way away and we all had to move again. This happened quite often.

Evenings often involved going to a show on the end of the pier. We once saw Frankie Vaughan singing Green Door. Such happy memories! To this day I love going on holiday, as do both my sister and brother.

David mostly travels abroad, whereas Kathleen and I enjoy our static caravans. Recently, David followed the family trend and purchased a Holiday Home in Mid-Wales.

Grandma Kynaston

When we lived in Newtown I would sometimes journey and stay with Grandma Kynaston in her little terraced cottage in Lower Brook Street, Oswestry. It was a two up and two down with no hot water or bathroom. The toilet was situated in a communal yard at the back and, as there was no bathroom, she would fill a tin bath in front of the fire for us to bathe in. The water came from a kettle she boiled on a black lead grate.

Grandma was also an excellent cook having run the Willow Cafe in Willow Street, Oswestry for many years. I don't know how she managed

it with no modern facilities. My memory is of some lovely dinners and junket for pudding, which was a type of blancmange made with rennet. I remember the kitchen in that house very well, with its large mangle in the corner!

For a treat we used to play on the Castle Bank in the middle of Oswestry. Once, a long time ago, a castle stood on the mound and defended the town forming an important link in the chain of Norman defence along the Welsh border. Now it is just ruins, but as children we would run up those circular paths to the top where the view was spectacular. No doubt it took Grandma a while to catch up with us!

Oswestry had an open-air market which, I believe, was where the National Westminster Bank is now. That was another place Grandma visited and they had live chickens for sale. I always felt sorry for them as the chickens had their legs tied together.

On Wednesdays, cows and sheep were herded through the streets on their way to the Cattle Market in the centre of town on English Walls. I always remember the mess that they left on the road. It's now the town's central car park, and it's hard to believe all the livestock that was bought and sold there at the auction.

Growing Up

In 1954, when I was fourteen years old, I had a Saturday job at Kay's Catalogue for four hours on a Saturday morning. I was paid two shillings an hour to pack leaflets in catalogues. It was good money then. When I was fifteen, Dad was promoted to Editor of the Border Counties Advertizer. This is when we moved to live in Oswestry. My parents bought a house on Victoria Road, just down the road from where my Grandma Kynaston lived.

Woodcote was a large five bedroomed black-and-white house with a tennis lawn and orchard at the back. For this beautiful house they paid £3,300 and that included the stable and garage.

My bedroom was huge and had a wash basin in it (no en-suites then). I loved this house. Some time after we moved in, to boost their income, Mum and Dad rented out a living room and a bedroom, sharing the kitchen. First, a couple named Rolly Jones and his wife Gladys moved in with us, and when they moved out another newly married couple came.

I went to Oswestry Girls High School, but didn't enjoy it much as I always felt like an outsider. I was short and the girls in my class seemed to tower over me. I did make some friends though. We spent a lot of our time talking rather than listening, and I wished I had paid more attention to my education. I would definitely know more now if I had.

My best friend was Margaret Lyon. I tasted my first cigarette when I pinched one from my Grandma Stott's packet while she was staying with us. My brother and I were walking to a friend's farm to see her pony when we stopped and I had a puff. It made me feel sick so consequently, I couldn't eat any of the tea I was offered at the farm. My next puff wasn't until a few years later when I was sixteen. My friend, Margaret Lyon and I had gone to Shrewsbury flower show, and she persuaded me to try one. We used to go swimming together at the public baths in Victoria Street on a Saturday morning. Afterwards, we would ride horses with Mr. Green who brought his ponies down to Oswestry from his riding stables in Selattyn. We would meet him in Weston Lane and from there would go for an hour ride.

Margaret lived with her parents in an upstairs flat in Lime Grove, Oswestry before they purchased a house at the bottom of College Road.

Family Pets &Work

It came to my knowledge that a family who lived in a large house just before Oswestry Racecourse, known as Oerley Hall, were looking for someone to exercise their two ponies, as their daughters were away at boarding school. I offered and went to ride the larger one whose name was Sabroon. He was a fifteen hand grey gelding. The smaller one was called Melody, who was about fourteen hands. I loved cycling up there and the family were very kind to me.

Whilst visiting the ponies I heard about a nanny goat kid just a few days old, which the farm over the road wanted to find a home. As we had a large garden, I persuaded Mum to let me have her. I called her Jane, but she later became known as Jinny. She was a Saanan, which is pure white, but after having her for a couple of years we rehomed her. We received an amazing thirty-one replies to our advert in the Advertizer.

We chose a family who lived high on a hill above Newtown where we thought was the most suitable. It was not too far from where we used to live in Newtown. The hamlet was called Llanchwchairn. I did miss Jinny, but some years later bought another goat.

I also did a bit of babysitting for Dad's boss, Mr. Eric Thomas, who had three daughters. He owned Woodall's Newspapers and lived in a large detached house on Morda Road in Oswestry. I would sleep overnight and was paid very well, which was nice. I also babysat for the daughter of one of Dad's colleagues.

When I was sixteen years old, I was still mad about horses and found Mr. Edwards, who had a farm in Weston Lane, Oswestry and was a horse dealer. He had a lovely thirteen hand bay pony called Cindy and I desperately wanted her. She was £38 and Mum asked Mr. Edwards if he would accept monthly payments, which he agreed to do. What he didn't tell me was that she was what was called broken-winded. This meant the horse had an airway obstruction. I didn't know what it was until I came to sell her, although I knew she panted when galloping. She was very keen and very fast. The faster she went, the more she would grunt.

Initially, I kept her on our large lawn and in the stable, but after a while rented a field at Mile House Farm where the golf course is today. For some of the rent, I cleaned their show ponies' stables.

Mr. and Mrs. Thompson, the farm owners, were very kind to me. At one of Mum's garden parties, I gave pony rides. I also instructed riding lessons to one of Eric Thomas' daughters. I loved Cindy and had many hours of fun with her.

A funny incident happened some years later in the stable with my boyfriend Pat. He suspected there were rats in there and, as he had an air rifle, asked me to hold it while he raked amongst the straw. Just then a large rat came running out and, without thinking, I shot at it, just missing both Pat and the rat! It did result in Pat leaping high in the air. Had I not missed, we may not have had any children.

Although I loved Cindy, as soon as boys appeared on the scene I decided to sell her, and this was when I found out she was broken-winded. The people who bought her made us reduce the purchase price.

Kathleen

While writing these memoirs I must devote a chapter about my amazing sister Kathleen and her husband Keith.

Kathleen was five years older than me, so when we moved to Oswestry from Newtown she didn't join us. On leaving school Kathleen trained in childcare, first working at a children's home in Shrewsbury and then at Dr Barnardo's at Welwyn Garden City, near London. She had always had a love for children and whilst living in Newtown would regularly take the neighbour's children out for walks. One child was a two-year-old called Roger and another was Brian who was three. I used to accompany her and I suppose this was my initial contact with small children.

During her time at Dr Barnardo's she would often bring toddlers home with her for the weekend. Kathleen's boyfriend at the time was Keith Parry who was a postman in Chester. One day I can remember her telling my parents she was pregnant. A wedding was quickly arranged for November and I was to be bridesmaid. After their wedding Keith transferred to being a postman in Oswestry, where they set up home. On the 23rd April their daughter Karen was born and Simon followed a year later. When their two children were quite small, they decided to apply to become foster carers for Shropshire County Council. I very often helped them with the many children who arrived at their home, some only for a short time, but others for longer. For a while Kathleen also worked as a teacher in the nursery at Bellan House School where she would take Karen with her.

After a couple of years in Oswestry, Keith successfully applied to join Manchester City Police Force, so the family moved to Manchester; he also played in the Manchester Police Band as a cornet player. They were unable to take the two small boys they were already fostering, but Social Services agreed that my mother and father could become their carers. However, Mum's temperament was not suitable, so they did not stay with us very long which was a pity as they were dear little boys. I often wonder where the two boys are now.

After moving to Manchester they had two further daughters, Joanne and Amanda. They then applied to Manchester City Council to be approved again as foster carers. As well as bringing up their four, they fostered over 700 children, adopting five over a period of forty-seven years. They devoted their lives to caring for children.

Soon after moving to Manchester a little girl of two years old arrived, and they cared for her long-term until adulthood. Her name was Susie. She became very friendly with Julie, the eldest of our three long-term sisters, and are still in touch even now they are in their forties.

Many children came and went after Susie and in the early 1980s, they fostered their first special needs little boy who was three years old. He lived with them until his death at the age of twenty-five years. Nicholas was blind and suffered from hydrocephalus. He had to be fed through a tube in his stomach. Nicholas couldn't see but, he could hear and he loved listening to music on tapes when he would rock to the rhythm. He could not speak. As he grew older and heavier they had a hoist installed as he was too heavy to lift.

While Nicholas was still young they were asked to care for another special needs child with multiple disabilities. Her name was Rebecca. Neither she, nor Nicholas, had any contact with their families. This meant they had two children in wheelchairs, which involved a lot of lifting so to help transportation they purchased a used minibus that seated twelve. Some years after caring for Rebecca, who they loved, they were approached by Social Services and asked if they would be interested in adopting her, which they said they would and were successful.

Unfortunately, Rebecca died just before her tenth birthday and they were devastated. Just before her death she had started to take a few steps with help.

Some years later Millie aged eighteen months and her four-year-old brother, Robert, joined the family. Shortly afterwards a baby brother, Richard, was born and he joined the family straight from the hospital. Kathleen and Keith decided to apply to adopt these three siblings and although they were over the age limit, because there being no other prospective adopters, they were successful.

As these three children grew more independent and Robert joined the army, they received a request to take a special needs four-month-old baby girl called Elizabeth with a rare life-limiting syndrome. She had severe curvature of the spine and, like Nicholas, had to be fed directly into her stomach. They grew to love Elizabeth. She was a very sensitive child and disliked loud noises or anyone shouting and would cry easily, so Kathleen would start singing to her, which soon had her smiling again.

Kathleen always gave me good advice, and I regularly rang her to discuss any problems I had. She had a wicked sense of humour and often had me crying with laughter. I never remember them asking for respite, although Kathleen suffered with asthma attacks. When these attacks were particularly bad, she would have to stay in bed while Keith took over. Occasionally, this would involve a short stay in hospital. Luckily by this time Keith had taken early retirement from the Police Force. He was a tremendous help and it became a joint effort.

By this time Kathleen and Keith had extended their home and exchanged their elderly minibus for a more modern vehicle which had an electric ramp and lift. This made life much easier. They regularly travelled to their holiday caravan, first being near Aberystwyth, then Borth, and finally in Anglesey. This latest caravan was situated all on its own overlooking Holyhead Bay where the ferries travel back and forth to Ireland. The caravan had a large garden where they put swings and a climbing frame. They also took two dogs with them. At first the site owner did not want them to replace the two-bedroom caravan, but when he met the children they cared for he changed his mind. They were able to purchase a caravan with four bedrooms, which was very unusual.

Any time a new event occurred, I had to tell Kathleen straight away, as we lived quite a long way from each other. I never remember her saying she was too busy to talk, which I am sure she was on occasions. She always gave me good advice. Having two children in wheelchairs required full-time care and a lot of lifting was involved, especially when staying in their caravan. This was particularly difficult as Kathleen sometimes had breathing problems, but this did not stop her from continuing caring.

As Elizabeth grew older she learnt to communicate by computer. She was not expected to have a long life. As Kathleen and Keith became frustrated with all the meetings with Social Services, they decided to try and adopt her. They applied and again were successful. They continued to care for numerous toddlers in addition to Elizabeth, and in fact were caring for two short stay children right up to a month before their deaths.

At the age of seventy-four, Keith was diagnosed with pancreatic cancer. After this, Kathleen's health deteriorated. Devastated at the news, I think she lost the will to live and couldn't face life without him.

At one time Keith was in hospital in a ward upstairs and Kathleen in a ward on the ground floor. The two babies had to be moved and the older children cared for Elizabeth.

Keith died a month before his seventy-fifth birthday in August 2010 and a month later Kathleen passed away with her three daughters by her side, also a month before her seventy-fifth birthday.

Joanne had flown in from America and with the help of the other three children, they looked after Elizabeth. The only problem was because of her severe disabilities, none of them could care for her on a long-term basis.

Joanne had to return to her life in America, and both Karen and Amanda worked full time. Luckily, with the help of Social Services, a residential home near to Karen was found for Elizabeth where she is very happy and has exceeded all expectations. Elizabeth celebrated her 21st birthday in 2016. Her family keep in touch and visit when they can. Elizabeth also attended the weddings of Karen`s two children, accompanied by her carer.

I can remember where I was when I learned of Kathleen's death. I was sitting outside our vets and couldn't believe I had lost my amazing sister. Although we hadn't lived together since we were young, Kathleen and I had the same views and outlook on life, and even our taste in clothes was the same. Even now I think of something I would love to tell her and have one of our long conversations, but of course, I can't anymore.

I know how difficult it must have been for Kathleen and Keith's children losing both parents so close together. I met Kathleen's and Keith's three daughters a year later in Anglesey to scatter their ashes around their caravan, which the two of them had loved. I still miss Kathleen and nobody can take her place.

Boyfriends and the Future

There was a boy called Derek who I fancied, but much to my disappointment he showed no interest in me. I thought he was good-looking and would visit venues where I thought he would be, all to no avail. However, some years later I saw him in Oswestry and couldn't understand what I had seen in him.

Another boy was doing some building work at the wholesale newspapers where I worked. Despite smiling sweetly at him, he didn't respond. I can remember sitting at the edge of the dance floor at the Victoria Rooms, which was quite near our house in Woodcote, and waited self-consciously to be asked to dance. Occasionally, I was asked to dance.

The time came for me to leave school and I had no clue as to what career I wanted to pursue. I applied to attend a childcare course, but it was oversubscribed and I wasn't successful.

My experience with boys was quite limited. I had had a few casual ones, but nothing serious. There was one particular boy who slobbered when we kissed, so he had to go. Then there was a lovely quiet boy called Malcolm, but he was rather boring, so I ended it.

My best friend, Margaret was corresponding with a boy from Belgium and he had a friend called Domien. It was arranged for me to write to him. He was studying in college and eventually continued on to university. Margaret's friend was training to be a test pilot. After corresponding for some time, they exchanged photographs.

I lived for these letters to arrive. I think Domien was my first love. When the lads informed us they would be visiting Leicester, we couldn't contain our excitement. Dad agreed to take us there to meet them.

On meeting Domien, I fell in love and it was arranged for them to come to Oswestry. I am a complete sucker for a continental accent. We walked hand in hand in Oswestry Cae Glas Park and Domien carved a heart on one of the tree trunks, all very romantic. I'm sorry to say that some years later I could find no sign of it. After they returned to Belgium, we continued our letters, which I kept. Owing to the distance involved, the romance fizzled out, but he certainly was my first real love.

Margaret's friend always said he would die young. I don't know whether this was because he was a test pilot. Sadly, his prophecy rang true and he died in a plane crash at an early age.

Dad arranged for me to work at Morris' wholesale newspapers as a clerk and I liked the girl I worked with, Alma. I earned £3 a week of which I gave Mum £1.50 for my board and lodgings. However, after twelve months Mrs. Morris decided she couldn't keep me. Dad recommended it would be good for me to attend a secretarial course at Shrewsbury Technical College. It was a nine-month intensive course involving shorthand, typing, English and Law.

I caught a bus from outside Wynne Roberts Newsagents in Salop Road. I loved going to college and discovered I was good at shorthand and typing. The teachers treated us as adults, so different from my school experiences. I especially loved typing to music and became quite proficient.

I finished my course with a diploma and accepted a job as junior clerk at Oswestry Rural District Council. I gained a level 3 RSA typewriting with credit and 120 words a minute shorthand. I think the fact that my father was friendly with Mr. Dillwyn David, Clerk to the Council, also helped.

My first assignment was to type an Abstract of Accounts, which was quite daunting. Talk about being thrown in at the deep end! I also had to type Mr. David's letters and deal with mortgages and small lotteries. I was later promoted to Mr. David's Secretary. He was a nice boss but suffered from a bad back, and while dictating his letters would moan about his back. While working at the Council, I worked closely with Mr. David`s deputy, Mr. Norman Evans. He dictated letters, which I recorded in shorthand and typed. I got on very well with him.

Sometimes Mr. Evans and I would be sent to help on election days and on one occasion we were being driven to the venue by Mr. Evans' wife. She casually stated that her husband suffered from piles, which was rather embarrassing for both myself and Mr. Evans.

At this point I was married and Patrick and I were expecting our first child the following February so I left the council in November 1966 to begin my maternity leave . The council staff were attending their Christmas meal at a local hotel. I later heard that Mr. Norman Evans, deputy clerk to the Rural District Council, had failed to show up at the hotel although his car was still parked nearby. Even his wife had no clue to his whereabouts. It was a complete mystery to everyone and to this day, over fifty years later, he has never been found.

Marriage

While I was still corresponding with Domien, I was waiting for the bus one early summer morning, and popped into the newsagents to buy some sweets. The young lad serving behind the counter said to me, "What are you doing buying cough sweets at this time of the year?"

Little did I know he would later become my husband! When I told my friend Margaret I fancied the boy in the newsagents, she said, "Oh! He's a friend of my boyfriend, John. I'll ask him to arrange a blind-date for us all to go to the pictures if you want?" So, all four of us visited the cinema one evening. The funny thing was that Pat had no idea who his date was until I turned up.

From then on, we saw each other regularly, often going for bike rides as Pat was a keen cyclist and rode in races. Other times we would listen to records in his Mum's front room.

Pat was an only child as his sister had died of a hole in the heart at the age of thirteen. She had been scheduled to have an operation, but fell ill before it could take place. His father had died at an early age when Pat was five, and his mother went on to remarry a lovely man named George Edge.

Pat was learning the guitar and would strum along to the records. In those days we both enjoyed a cigarette and sometimes would share one. His mum always rattled the door knob before coming into the front room. I don't know what she expected us to be doing, but she was very tactful. She would cook us large suppers, which I loved usually involving chips. Sunday tea was always a big salad. She always had a cigarette in her mouth while preparing this and I dreaded the ash falling into the food!

After Pat and I married she gave us bacon, biscuits, butter and other treats every week which certainly helped the housekeeping. We went on holiday three times before we were married. The first was a week in Southsea, then a few days in Llandudno and finally ten days (our first trip abroad) in Diana Marina in Italy, which cost us twenty-nine and a half guineas.

We had to travel overnight to the continent sleeping in the coach and the same on the way back. It probably wasn't very comfortable, but being young and in love, it didn't matter. When we journeyed to Llandudno, we travelled on Pat's Aerial Leader motorbike with an extremely large suitcase on the back, which in hindsight, was probably dangerous. When we arrived at the hotel, they put us in a double room and innocently we informed them that we weren't married. They then gave us two singles. I am not saying there wasn't a bit of visiting between rooms!

I was dating Pat and at the age of twenty-one we were engaged. I can't remember him going down on one knee, but I chose a ring with a ruby surrounded by diamonds.

By this time my parents were living in a bungalow they had built next door to Woodcote. They had decided the house was too big and had a bungalow built on the tennis court in the garden. My parents called it Meadowlea.

After we had been engaged for eighteen months, Grandma Kynaston could no longer care for herself and moved in with my parents, so the wedding was brought forward as space was tight.

The wedding date of Saturday 7th September 1963 was arranged. The wedding was to be in our church, Oswald Road Presbyterian at twelve noon. My bridesmaids were my cousin Gillian, Pat's cousin, Janet, and my two smaller bridesmaids were Karen, my niece, and Christine, Pat's cousin. The reception was held at the Masonic Hall in Roft Street. Our honeymoon was spent in Torquay.

Dad was a public relations officer at the Orthopaedic hospital and so asked the chef who was in charge to provide the food, but never discussed what it would cost. I must admit the food was gorgeous, but Dad did turn pale when he received the bill.

The buffet meal comprised of salmon, chicken, prawns, beef and other delicious delicacies. I had a beautiful dress of Nottingham lace, which I hired from a firm in Manchester. The two elder bridesmaids wore lilac and the two younger ones, apple green. Unfortunately, the drive to the bungalow had yet to be finished, so I had to walk the plank to the car that was transporting me and Dad.

My bouquet was a bunch of deep red roses, which were identical to the bouquet that my mother had carried on her wedding day. The morning of the wedding proved to be very wet, but I didn't care and enjoyed it all.

We hired an Austin mini from a local firm to travel to Torquay. We had both passed our driving test, me on the second occasion, but still only owned a motorbike.

On arriving at our hotel late in the evening, it was to be the first time we'd shared a double bed. Next morning it turned out that all the staff knew we were on our honeymoon.

At the end of the week away, we decided to go on a fishing trip, but this turned out to be a bad idea as we both were really sick due to a rough sea. I also left my lovely white jacket on the back of a deckchair. We had to return home on the Friday as my friend Val, who worked with me at the council, was getting married a week after us on the following Saturday.

Our First Homes, Caravans & Boats

To start our married life, we purchased a static caravan for £500, which we had sited at the back of Meadowlea in the Orchard. It had two bedrooms, a kitchen, bathroom and living area with an outside balcony. It also had a solid fuel fire and central heating. I loved it.

This started a long and happy love for caravanning, which continued in 1965 when we purchased our first touring caravan, a ten-foot long Bluebird, which we towed behind Pat's Mini Cooper. Many more touring caravans and static holiday homes came and went with a change which seemed to happen every three or four years, right up until 2012 when we purchased our current holiday home.

Unfortunately, after we had been married for three months, our first Christmas was spent apart except for tea. Pat had to go into the Cottage hospital to have his appendix removed. I thought it was my cooking! After splitting open his scar from coughing, Pat gave up smoking and hasn't smoked since. I continued smoking one or two a day but tried not to inhale, eventually giving up completely.

We then moved to a second floor flat on Salop Road, Oswestry for which we paid £2 a week. The house was owned by a Mr. Evans, a retired dentist and his wife who lived on the ground floor. The first floor was let to another couple. It had one large living room, a big bedroom, and the kitchen, where the bath was housed under a work surface. There was no toilet on our floor, and we had to share one with the flat on the floor below.

We had two poodles, Tina who was white and Candy black. Luckily the landlord allowed us to take them. Mr. and Mrs. Evans had a daughter

Faith and a son, Sam. Some years after my father retired, Sam became editor of the Advertizer.

After about eighteen months at the flat, we moved to a terraced cottage on New Park Road at an increased rent of £8 a week. It had a kitchen, living room and two bedrooms, but no bathroom. Also, there was a long back garden, so while visiting Kathleen in Manchester we went to a market and ended up buying some little chicks. They were lovely little yellow balls of fluff. We patiently waited for them to grow big enough to produce some fresh eggs for breakfast. However, they became quite vicious and only then did we discover they were all cockerels. An elderly neighbour offered to kill them for us but, when it came to eating them, we just couldn't and ended up giving them away. After being in New Park Road we then found a semi-detached house in Queens Road which cost us £15 a month, it had five bedrooms over three storeys but no central heating. To reach the bathroom I had to go through one of the bedrooms. I certainly didn't linger long in the bath or I would have had frostbite, as often there was ice on the inside of the windows. Even though we had three coal fires, the house was still cold in the winter.

Pat had been left a semi-detached bungalow in his Grandmother's will, but her sister had the right to live in the property and we couldn't have it until both sisters had died. These two sisters had run this bungalow as a post office for many years and after his Grandmother's death, Aunty Zillah lived there alone. She was unmarried and was a very keen Girl Guider in her younger days. When she passed away in 1968, we used the proceeds to put a deposit on our first home in Prince Charles Close.

It cost £2,900 and had a corner plot making a lovely large garden. As it was situated in a cul-de-sac we thought it would be ideal for us having two small children, and a year later we added a garage.

Whilst living in Prince Charles Close myself and other ladies who were neighbours with small children, would meet for coffee in each other's houses. Next door lived Lorraine and Mark, and twice a week I would day-mind her son while she worked. I think I earned about 50p a session. I expect it would be a bit more these days!

After some time meeting in houses, we began meeting in a cafe for coffee, eventually moving to lunch and finally, as the children grew older we meet for an evening meal, once a month. We are not all neighbours any more as some have moved to other areas of Oswestry.

Forty-five years later we still meet monthly although now we are all grannies. There are ten of us with a few joining along the way. We usually meet at the Sweeney Hotel just out of Oswestry and rarely drink alcohol. Sean, the owner treats us very well.

After a few years we moved from Prince Charles Close to a new build around the corner. We needed a bigger house as we had just been approved as foster carers. Middleton Road was a country lane back then. We put in an offer, moved in, and still live there today.

We did have a nasty incident when one evening Pat had gone to play squash and I had prepared tea for when he returned. I had put fish fingers under the grill and chips in the chip pan and went to talk to Kathleen on the phone. I completely forgot about the food. When I opened the lounge door to go back to the kitchen, a wall of heat met me. The whole back of the house was filled with dense smoke. I phoned the fire brigade and then ran to get the baby from the cot upstairs. They arrived and all these firemen filled my house. Pat received a message from our neighbour to say there was a fire and as he was playing squash with a doctor, the doctor came too. Luckily nobody was hurt, but the smell

40

throughout the house was terrible and everywhere, except the lounge, was smoke damaged. It was a terrible shock and taught me a lesson.

Everywhere was redecorated under the house insurance. Some months after the fire I felt as though there was something sharp in my throat when swallowing. My doctor sent me to the Eye, Ear and Throat Hospital in Shrewsbury and I had to have an operation. I am not sure what they removed or whether it was connected to the fire, but it certainly felt like broken glass.

During the many happy years of caravanning we also enjoyed a number of extremely enjoyable holidays boating with our friends Mary, Garry, and their children. This started in 1979 when we both hired a private sixty foot canal boat at Welsh Frankton boat yard. The following two years also saw both families hiring boats on the Leeds-Liverpool canal at Skipton in Yorkshire. In 1981, we were very fortunate to be offered a free canal boating holiday by the owners of Black Prince Canal Boating company at Whixall Moss Marina. The owners Mr.& Mrs. Rimmer, who we met at frequent fostering events, admired the work we were doing with young children. The couple offered ourselves and Mary's family two boats for a week to travel the Shropshire and Cheshire canal system. A great time was had by all. The children of both families really enjoyed all the lock work and walking the dogs up and down the towpath.

After we had bought our second static caravan, we became involved in more exciting boating by purchasing a twenty-three foot Swedish built Morbas sea boat. This was kept in the harbour at Aberystwyth and over the next nine years was upgraded or changed three times. We eventually sold our last boat and reverted back to touring with a caravan in 1997. Many happy hours were involved in "mucking" about in boats with the children. We always enjoyed the adventures regardless of whether it was on canal holidays, the Norfolk Broads, or in the coastal waters from Aberystwyth into Cardigan Bay and the Irish Sea. We always had a family policy that whoever was in our care at the time of any holidays always came with us. Often, children from the age of six months up to twenty years would join in the holiday adventures. These adventures created lasting memories for the children in our care.

Pets Galore

Over the years, we have had numerous pets, not counting the chickens. I mentioned my first goat and pony, but we also had a Minah bird, which would throw its fruit all over the wallpaper. We have had rabbits, a cockatoo, and a Senegal parrot named Oswald. There were lots of guinea pigs, and even a salamander lizard that lived in a tank under the stairs.

As a child whilst living in Chester my first pet was a Springer Spaniel

named Sally, but my mother was not very fond of her and she had to be rehomed. A few years later we acquired a cocker spaniel named Bruce. He was a lovely golden and white colour.

My two miniature poodles, Candy and Tina were very sweet. Candy was always nervous and Tina was just the opposite. I'd acquired them before I was married. They died of old age around the time our daughter was born.

It was so awful without a dog that when Lisa was six months old we went to Nottingham, ninety miles away and purchased a pale-yellow Labrador puppy. We named her Elsa after watching the lioness in the film Born Free. Elsa lived until the age of eleven.

Many more followed including a German shepherd named Sheba, two Yorkshire Terriers named Tara and Heidi, a Lassie collie named Gemma, a Sheltie named Hannah, a Pekinese named Daisy, and numerous cats.

On one occasion, we were on our way to a static caravan we owned near Aberystwyth when we realised we had left Heidi at home by mistake, so we had to return home to collect her!

Elsa

Sheba with Nick and Adam

Animals have always played a big part in our lives and we have had all different types, such as horses, dogs, goats, fish, mice, parrots, etc. We had free-range guinea pigs on our back lawn for over twenty years.

Not many people realise that guinea pigs do not run away, but will happily return to their cage when allowed to roam free. The very last guinea pig we had was very old and rather than having to ask friends to feed it when we were away at our caravan, I purchased a cage to leave there permanently.

We took the guinea pig in a carrying case and reached our caravan, but on lifting her out she dropped down dead. I think her time had come, but a shame she never made it to her lovely new holiday home.

When I had my first goat, we decided to put her in kid, so we could have milk. We borrowed Dad's Triumph Herald to take her to Minsterley where an old man had a Billy goat. We put the back seat flat, but unfortunately, Jinny peed all down it and Dad was not very pleased!

When we reached the farm, the man brought the Billy out, gave it a

Lisa Humby with the three kids.

kick up the bum and this very smelly goat jumped on our goat for all of two seconds. We presumed it was too quick to have mated. Lo-and-behold, five months later after we had sold her, she produced kids. I couldn't believe it could happen that quickly!

The second goat I obtained was a nanny who I bought from a dealer, but when we arrived home, I just couldn't milk her. She kept kicking the bucket over. There was a vet at the time on Radio 2 who would offer advice on any problems listeners had with their pets. I rang the programme, and it went on air. He gave me good advice, but I am afraid I still couldn't get the knack of milking her, and had to return her to her former owner who said the kid would be pleased to get his mum back.

Some years later I finally managed to milk a goat when we purchased another. The next goat I acquired was named Kizzy, and Pat built me an enclosure which surrounded part of the garden where her shed was.

Some days I took her down the lane to an orchard where I was allowed to tether her during the day and collect her every evening. One day she stopped to nibble a hedge opposite our house and the owner shouted at me.

45

I would pick branches from the lane we lived on and Kizzy loved these. She was a real pet and provided the family with milk. I even sold some to a lady who had a child with bad skin. Goat's milk is excellent for skin disorders. We made yoghurt from her milk, too. So for many years we didn't buy milk, although the children moaned about having to drink goat's milk as it has a stronger taste than cow's milk.

Kizzy was a brown Toggenburg goat. Later we bought Katy who was black and white. When we went on holiday, a lady would come and take them both to her farm over the old racecourse. One of her kids was called Posie, and we later learned she had been made a champion at an agriculture show.

On one occasion we entered them in Oswestry agricultural show, which was great fun. Kizzy gave birth to triplets, and they had their photograph in the Advertizer.

We have no goats now, but they are lovely animals. It is a myth that they will eat anything. In fact, they are very fussy and won't even touch bread that has been on the ground. I think it is because they like to nibble things.

One adventure I remember involved cats. Before we had our children, we had gone with Kathleen and her family to a remote cottage on the banks of Loch Tummel near Pitlochry in Scotland. We set off really early, but their ancient car broke down delaying us for four hours while it was being mended.

The cottage was situated in the most picturesque spot, but was quite primitive. We discovered a family of feral cats who were extremely pretty and long haired. Every day we enticed them with food trying to coax them into the cottage and eventually they entered, but all hell let loose. What we hadn't realised was that they were wild.

They went ballistic and ran up the walls. Pat, bless him, built a makeshift cage to transport the cats home. We found a home for one with the mother of a girl I worked with (she, in fact, had it for over fifteen years) and we kept the other one. They were really beautiful Persians.

Over the years we have found homes for numerous animals including a German shepherd from Manchester who went to a colleague of mine, and a Yorkshire terrier from Aberystwyth, who went to a girlfriend and her family.

Before we had children, I had visited kennels near to where Kathleen lived and I came home with a Yorkshire terrier puppy. I hadn't told Pat and he was really upset and wouldn't speak to me for a while, but did let me keep her. Unfortunately, some time later I had tied her to the gear stick in my car as I didn't want her jumping through the open window while I did my shopping. To my horror when I returned I discovered she had managed to jump through and hung herself by her lead. It was awful, and I was very upset at my stupidity.

We didn't plan on having four cats, but when we found a female with kittens in one of the buildings on our caravan site, we brought her and her kittens home.

We kept the mother cat and called her Abbey as she had been found in Aberystwyth and found homes for the kittens. She often accompanied us back up to the caravan. We also took a beautiful grey cat called Murphy who came from a farm belonging to a boyfriend of one of the girls.

Unfortunately, one day when Murphy was still young he went missing. After searching for days and putting up adverts, we decided he had gone for good. Every time we read an advert for a cat that had been found we would build our hopes up only to be disappointed again. We always knew

 how we would know it was him as he had a nasty scar where he had been knocked down by a car not long before.

After Murphy didn't turn up, my daughter Lisa came home with a grey female cat to replace him. We called her Lottie. Something rather funny happened one day with her.

My neighbour came round to say she had seen a lady putting Lottie into her car outside our house. We rushed out and asked the lady what she was doing, to which she replied that Lottie was her lost cat. She was absolutely convinced and to settle the argument, we had to take Lottie to our vet to confirm she was female, as the lady's cat was male. Only then did she accept that Lottie was ours. After Murphy had been missing for eight months our neighbour, Olive, saw an advert seeking the owner of a grey cat that had been found. As it was about four miles away at Park Hall, we didn't think for one minute it could be Murphy, but we went anyway. To our absolute amazement, it was indeed Murphy.

He happily hopped into our car as he had regularly travelled in it to our static caravan. We were delighted to have him home, but it did mean we now had four cats. The only thing we think happened was that children had carried him away and he couldn't find his way back. Either that, or he had climbed into someone's car.

Murphy had, I think, lived on rabbits in the area of Park Hall camp and had also been fed by workmen who had a hut near this lady's house. When this was removed he obviously went to her house, and it was then that she put an advert into the local paper. It was such a happy story that he was featured in an article in the paper, along with his photograph.

We borrowed trekking ponies for the winter months for three years running from 1981, which turned out to be one of the coldest for many

48

years. The third winter we had a Dun mare, who was lovely but not a novice ride. One day, Adam decided he was going to have a ride on her, but he couldn't ride very well and lost control. We watched in terror as she took off down the road with him hanging on for grim death. To his credit he didn't fall off and managed to stop her, to our relief.

In 1991, after a break from horses, Lisa and I decided to borrow two for the winter from a lady who ran a trekking stables some miles from Oswestry. We enjoyed riding these ponies and kept them in a field near Ellesmere.

One day I had a nasty accident when riding down a country lane. The girth on my saddle broke causing me to fall forward. The horse also fell, and I cut my chin on the concrete. I sat there grateful to be alive, but I was in shock and asked Lisa to phone her dad. Thank God for mobile phones. He arrived to take me home; however, as I was injured, he decided I should go to the Orthopaedic Hospital. They examined me and x-rayed my hand, but after cleaning me up, the doctors let me return home. It wasn't only me who had been hurt; the horse received cuts on both her nose and legs, but made a full recovery.

That evening we were having our friends, Mary and Garry to a meal and I had prepared beef and Yorkshire pudding, so I didn't want to cancel. They were shocked when they saw the state of my face. The following day we received a telephone call from the hospital informing us that when a doctor had another look at the x-rays of my hand, there was a tiny bone that needed to be repaired.

I had the operation while awake, but my arm was numb. Chris de Burgh was singing 'Lady in Red' in the theatre. The surgeon drilled into my hand and suddenly I had a sharp pain which made me jerk my arm. The surgeon shouted at me and said he was using very sharp instruments. I made sure I didn't move again. I was in a lot of pain after the operation as I had two wires sticking out of my hand. I was discharged after a couple of days, but told to return sometime later when they would remove the wires.

They told me it wouldn't hurt when I had the wires removed, but it was the most painful experience. A rather large nurse had to pull really hard until eventually the wires came out.

I felt ill after the procedure and as I had gone on my own. I don't know how I drove home. I made sure the surgeon knew how painful it had been when weeks later I had an appointment with him, to which he replied, "Well you must have very strong bones."

Family

After working in the newsagents and attending night school in accountancy, Pat obtained a job as a trainee accountant working at Jones and Co. Corn and Seed Merchants on English Walls, in Oswestry. After he gained his qualifications at night school he went to work for The Hospital Management Group in Shrewsbury. This is where he was working when we married. After two years he obtained the position of Payroll Manager with West Shropshire Water Board, later to be called Severn Trent Water.

While we lived in New Park Road I found out, to my delight, that I was pregnant with the baby being due February 1967. As we were expecting, we decided to move to a better house and moved to Queens Road, which cost us £15 a month to rent. We moved in before the baby was born. It had three large reception rooms, but no central heating. It was a bit cold, to say the least. I would light one or two fires using firelighters and newspaper to keep us warm.

When I was seven months pregnant, I caught flu and suffered a very high temperature. Pat contacted the doctor, but was told the baby would be fine and told me to drink lots of fluids. However, a month before my due date I began having labour pains, and the baby was showing signs of distress. Dr Hodnet sent me to The Royal Shrewsbury Hospital, and although I had had the usual check-ups, nobody noticed anything wrong. They listened to the heartbeat from time to time, but then informed me that my baby had died. I then had to go through labour and after thirty-six hours of pain I had a normal delivery, but didn't want to see my baby boy. Mum and Kathleen did see him and said he looked perfect. The first question I asked was, "How soon can I try for another one?"

When I arrived home, Pat had moved all baby things out of sight. The worst part was meeting people who all seemed to know someone who had lost a baby and saying, "It probably happened for the best." I am convinced now that it shouldn't have happened. They should not have left me when they knew the baby was distressed.

Luckily, I became pregnant almost straight away and the baby was due exactly twelve months after the first. I didn't go back to work and the due date soon arrived. I again suffered thirty-six hours of labour but to my great joy, I gave birth to a beautiful baby girl. Lisa Kate had dark hair and as soon as she arrived looked around the room as though she had been there before.

I loved being a mum, but it came as a bit of a shock to find some months later I was pregnant again. Lo and behold, this baby was also due in February. On the 21st of February in1969, Nicholas Patrick Ambrose arrived. This time I had been induced as he was overdue, but again it took yet another thirty-six hours. Life was rather hectic with a newborn and a toddler, but I loved it.

As my parents grew older they became more reliant on me, especially as Dad`s failing eyesight prevented him from driving. Mum also eventually gave up driving when her condition deteriorated. I used to take them shopping or to attend appointments.

One evening I received the call I had been dreading for years. Dad, who was then eighty-three years, had a nasty pain that wouldn't subside. We called for an ambulance and I stayed with Mum while Pat accompanied him to Shrewsbury hospital. Unfortunately, Dad died a little later in hospital with Pat by his bedside.

I brought Mum to our house, but owing to her state of mind she didn't really understand that Dad had died. Mum lived with us until a couple of weeks before she died, the day after my fifty-first birthday, at the age of eighty-seven. I was glad I was able to care for her even though I was also looking after a one-year-old. It was okay at first, but became quite challenging as her Alzheimer's got worse. She had done so much for us over the years that it was unthinkable not to care for her in the last years of her life.

I think the reason my father lived to the age of eighty-three after suffering with his heart for so long was due to the fact that he was very careful with his diet and didn't smoke or drink alcohol.

I can remember on one occasion we took Mum with us to our static caravan in Aberystwyth, she got up and opened the door and shouted for help and to call the Police. It was rather embarrassing until I explained. Thankfully our neighbours understood.

There were so many instances where my family gave back to the community. Besides all of the charities and organizations my parents belonged to, Pat and I also followed in their footsteps, using our family to help other families. For many years, Pat and I delivered and collected Christian Aid envelopes during the month of May. After collecting them Pat would count all the money before paying it into a special account for the Christian Aid organisation. This involved a lot of walking, which I enjoyed. It was interesting visiting other people's houses.

Pat was also the church treasurer and among other duties he had to count and bank the contents of the Sunday collection and any other payments received by the church.

Once a year, Pat visited the Severn Trent Water Authority retired employees and I accompanied him. This was to check if they were ok or had any questions about their pensions. I enjoyed travelling and sometimes these visits took us as far as Llanidloes. Any child I was looking after would also come with us. Just as my parents showed me the beauty in giving back to others, I hoped to impress upon the children the importance of it as well.

Transport and Making Ends Meet

As I said earlier, we didn't have a car when we first married, only several motorbikes (Not all at one time!). The first car we purchased was a black Ford Popular, which we bought from our friends Pauline and Len for the price of £50. We gave them £25 and borrowed £25 from our parents.

The next car we bought was a new Morris 1100, because Pat was involved in Motor Sport - rallying, driving tests and production car trials.

We then bought a fast, new Mini Cooper, which we took on many car competitions as members of Welsh Border Car Club and the Ellesmere Motor Club. Pat was secretary of the Ellesmere club and would often compete in or marshal and organise rallies, which were often held on a Saturday night.

One Sunday I entered a road safety competition, and I had to reverse up to a wall. By a sheer fluke and shouting by my husband, I reversed to within half an inch of the wall. I came first and had my photograph in the local Advertizer.

While we were emptying Aunty Zillah's bungalow, we found a box full of letters written by Ambrose, Pat's grandfather. A lot of them were written while he was courting his girlfriend Mabel, before they got engaged and many more while he was abroad during the First World War. Unfortunately, he was killed on active service in France while in the Royal Flying Corps. The letters were written right up to when the Air Force wrote to his widow Mabel informing her of his death.

It was interesting to read what he had written about courting his girlfriend. His family lived in Llanrwst and he rode for miles on his bike just to see her. When they married they moved to Sudbury on Thames in the south of England.

Another box contained letters from Pat's father, John Ambrose Humby (known as Jack) who was in the Royal Air Force, which he had written when he was serving in the Second World War in India and Burma. Sadly, he also died as a result of injuries sustained on active service. Both Pat's grandfather and father were in their thirties when they passed away serving their country in both the first and second world wars.

It was sad reading about the conditions the men had to endure during the Great War of 1914-18. I felt I knew Ambrose very well through his letters and wished we had been able to meet him.

Both men died too young and Ambrose was buried in Wimeroux in France and no living relative had ever visited the grave until we did in 1991. It was emotional as we really felt we knew this man. Our son Nicholas also made the trip to Wimeroux some years later and paid his respects.

In his letters, Ambrose always referred to "little Jack," Pat's father, who was born after he had joined the Royal Flying Corps. In Jack's letters to Emily, his wife, he referred to Pat, his son. He also referred to little Rita, Pat's sister and it's sad to think she also died young. She had a brain haemorrhage and died in 1951, aged thirteen years. She was what was known then as a blue baby, which is now referred to as a baby born with a hole in the heart. These days she would have had a good chance of being cured by corrective surgery.

When I began driving my parents around after Dad's eyesight had deteriorated, he gave me his car and over a period we upgraded it for a younger model. The last new car I purchased was my green Peugeot 106 in 2002 and it is still going strong. It has cost me next to nothing in repairs.

Party Plan

A neighbour in our first home in Prince Charles Close was Anne, who lived two doors away with her husband Gerry and daughter Jane. She asked me if I would be interested in selling baby clothes in people's houses, known as Party-Plan.

We then moved on to holding parties for a company called Pippa Dee. They sold ladies garments and underwear, including a few children's clothes. They provided us with a case of sample garments and we would ask friends to hold a party. We then demonstrated the clothing and afterwards they could order any item they liked. To begin the party one of us would give an introductory speech explaining the procedure after which they could try the clothes on. We would then go round each customer to see if they wanted anything and also to ask if they would hold a party themselves. We certainly got around the area, sometimes travelling to Shrewsbury and into Powys.

We didn't have any problems booking parties either as ladies seemed to enjoy the social side of it. I certainly learnt how to deal with people, visiting small modest homes or lavish residences.

Suppers were supposed to be simple, but some hostesses put on a spread. I made many friends and gradually the amount of parties snowballed.

There were some funny moments. One time I asked one lady whether her mum wanted anything. She replied, "Oh no, that's my sister!" Another funny instance occurred in Morda. While I was talking, a lady in front of me was mouthing every word I said. It was off-putting, to say the least.

Delivery of the orders from the party would be about three weeks later when the hostess had to collect monies for the amount sold. As a thank you, they received commission based on sales.

Business became so good we decided to split up and manage our own parties. On a good night, I could earn anything from £30 to over a £100. My work fitted in well with looking after the family, as the majority of parties were held in the evening. It was rather annoying when some mothers left their children up. Children could be a nuisance. I can't understand why some people don't seem to have a regular bedtime for their children. Mine always went to bed around seven o'clock.

Sometimes I would say something to someone and then wish the floor would swallow me up. For instance, on one occasion, I held up one of our bras and by mistake said this is our bugger bra, instead of bigger bra. Everyone thought it very funny. I always gave the hostess a small thank you present in addition to the commission. Some ladies would hold at least two parties a year. It certainly was a good way to earn extra money.

I carried on holding parties for a few years and to this day people say hello who knew me through my Pippa Dee days. Some still even now have the clothes that I sold them.

Foster Caring

When my two children were aged three and four years, we considered applying to become foster carers like Kathleen and her husband Keith. The two of us knew a little about what was involved, having helped her on occasions. We felt we had something to offer and applied to Social Services.

Sometime later we had a visit from the Children's Officer, as it was known then, and decided to proceed. We filled in all the necessary forms giving two referees, one the Rev J Pryce-Williams our Minister at Oswald Road Church, where we married, and the other, Mr Dillwyn David, Clerk to Oswestry Rural District Council, who was my old boss. There wasn't any training involved then and it certainly wasn't like it is now.

After quite a while we received the letter telling us we had been approved, and eagerly awaited the phone call asking us to care for our first child.

We were still living in Prince Charles Close but realised we would need a larger house and put ours on the market. In the meantime, the phone rang asking us to take two small boys aged three and five. We asked when they would be arriving and were shocked to learn that they were with a social worker outside our house.

They had been made homeless, so both needed looking after until their parents found somewhere to live. The older boy had very long hair, which I decided to trim.

On a shopping trip to town a few days later with all the children, I met the boy's parents. The father smelled of alcohol, and in a threatening manner asked me who had cut his son's hair. Of course, not feeling very brave, I denied it, but he angrily took the boys from me. It's a wonder this incident didn't put me off fostering, but many other lovely children soon followed.

A more pleasant experience was when we took a nine-month little girl whose mother suffered from a long-term mental illness, with regular bouts of depression.

There are so many reasons why children come into care. It can be a loss of housing, domestic, physical or mental abuse. Very few children, if any, are orphans. Also, families can suffer financial problems that lead to children entering the foster care system.

However short a time a child enters the care system it can affect them. I know what I would have been like had I had to leave my family. It is sometimes frightening caring for other people's children, as it's such a responsibility. These children can arrive at your house with very little, and usually are not used to any kind of routine. They leave behind everything that is familiar: smells, family, toys and pets. Most people imagine they would be grateful to be in a lovely home, but that isn't always the case.

It can take varying amounts of time for a child to settle. Some are fine straight away which is a little worrying, but others can be withdrawn and don't show their true character until much later. My mother-in-law was a great help with babysitting and my Mum also helped me as she did all my mending.

After a few short placements, the house was sold. We had been disappointed once when the people buying ours decided to buy a new build on the estate where we were buying ours. Eventually, a man came along and bought it, but said he didn't like the decoration, which I thought was a bit rude.

Our new house was a new build on Middleton Road, close to where we lived. It was a country lane back then, and just before it was finished, Social Services asked us to take an eleven-year-old boy on a long-term placement. David would be our first child fostered long-term.

At the same time, Social Services asked if we would consider becoming *'Professional'* Foster carers. This meant taking a minimum of four children on an extended placement. We agreed, but only after we had moved from our house and David had settled.

David's mother had died and at present he was being cared for by his grandmother, who was elderly and finding it difficult to cope. He had older brothers and sisters who lived independently.

After considering this we agreed, but as our new house was yet to be completed, we all stayed with my mother-in-law. David was a lovely boy, and settled in well.

A few weeks later we moved in to our lovely new house, where we still live today. With four bedrooms, we had a lot more room, although we did miss our large garden. David lived with us until the age of fifteen, when he moved to live with one of his married sisters. Occasionally he would come and visit us, and is now a grandfather himself. Unfortunately, at the age of 50, we learned he'd had a stroke but is managing to cope.

Whilst David was with us, a few short-term children came and went for varying lengths of time. One little boy arrived with finger marks around his neck where his mother had tried to strangle him. He wasn't with us long and returned home. I am not sure what caused this terrible state of affairs, but his mother was so grateful she gave us a bunch of flowers for caring for her son during this difficult period in her life.

We had a little blond boy aged about four who would disappear behind the garden shed to do a pooh, which was rather frustrating. Another time we were asked if we could accommodate four sisters, and for a very short time we actually had nine children. These girls proudly informed me that they all had different fathers.

We did manage one day to take all nine of them into the countryside near Oswestry for a picnic. We sat by a stream only to be shouted at by the farmer for being on his land. He probably thought it was a Sunday school outing.

We regularly took seven children on holiday in our touring caravan. The older boys slept in a tent, while the other children slept in an inner tent in the awning. We managed well. Also, Pat and I often took three, sometimes four dogs, leaving the four cats in the cattery. This cost us more than the rent we paid for the caravan pitch.

One day, Social Services contacted us to ask if we could take a four-and-a-half-year-old boy named Adam. He had been locked in his house for his own protection while his father went out. When the boy found the door locked, he panicked and jumped out of the bedroom window. Luckily a bay window broke his fall and he wasn't badly hurt. He was only a month older than our son and stayed with us until the age of seventeen.

When Adam arrived, he couldn't run very well and was small for his age, but now as an adult is above average height. He recently moved to a house near to us and runs his own decorating business. Adam is an excellent father to his two children. I am quite amazed as to what he can remember even though he was so young when he arrived. Time and time again I am surprised as to what children can remember.

Recently Adam discovered, through a relation of his father, that he had two half-brothers. Before Adam was born, a previous partner of his father's had a boy and girl. Their mother tried to drown them in the bath. The girl died, but her brother survived. We believe their mother was admitted to a psychiatric hospital. The relation also told Adam he had another half-brother born to a previous partner of his father. Adam managed to trace the boy who survived the drowning, but as yet hasn't found his other brother. Recently, Adam discovered that a trust fund had been set up enabling him to put a deposit on his first home.

While with us he had no contact with his own mother, but regularly saw his father. At the time of his eighteenth birthday his mother got in touch with him through Social Services and they met, however it didn't turn out to be the happy reunion he had hoped for.

Another long-term child we were asked to look after was a pretty blonde five-year-old girl who had been physically abused. She was very withdrawn, and her first words to us were, "My mummy doesn't like me." Probably as a result, she had a terrible temper and twelve months later her two sisters also came into the care system.

Initially, her two sisters were fostered with a friend of mine, but when she became poorly they had to move on. I agreed to take them as I felt it would be nice for them all to be together. Unfortunately, they fought like cats and dogs, and although on more than one occasion I regretted my decision, I plodded on with them and now am so pleased I didn't give up. The eldest girl, Julie, stayed with us until she was twenty-five. We are still very much in touch and all three are excellent mothers.

The girls are now in their forties and live locally. They have always been musical with lovely singing voices. Emma, the middle girl, appeared on Matthew Kelly's "Stars in Your Eyes" with her best friend, who was also in care, as Shakespeare's Sister. I travelled to Granada Studios in Manchester to watch the programme being recorded. Unfortunately, Pat couldn't come as he was in the hospital about to have an operation. All the girls belonged to the Girls' Brigade. Julie became an officer of the Girls' Brigade. We are very proud of the three of them.

During this period with the three girls and Adam, we still had many changes in our family. As mentioned earlier, we regularly took our caravan touring round most of the British Isles from Scotland to Cornwall. It was a great way of spending holidays with a large family.

On one occasion, we stayed on a beautiful site called Morfa Bychan, four miles out of Aberystwyth on the cliffs above the sea. Kathleen had a static caravan on this site and we decided that we would like to change our tourer and buy a static there. It proved wonderful for the children, who could run free and make friends while staying there.

There was a swimming pool in which they spent many a happy hour, and occasionally in the evening we would go to social events in the club on site. The girls loved performing on stage, and it certainly helped caring for them on long school holidays.

Pat joined us when he could, as at this time he was still working at Severn Trent Water Authority in Shrewsbury and Birmingham. After a couple of years, we swapped the caravan for a larger more comfortable one, eventually purchasing a beautiful twelve-foot-wide one with three bedrooms. In fact, we were the first family to have a new twelve-foot-wide caravan on this site. Of course, there are now many such caravans. We ordered it at the Caravan and Camping Show held every year at the NEC in Birmingham.

Often parents, accompanied by social workers, travelled to Aberystwyth for contact with their children. I remember we were caring for a three-year-old boy and a social worker brought along his four siblings. They had a lovely time playing on the swings and swimming in the pool. Happy days!

Once when the older girls began working, we could leave them at home. On one occasion we received a phone call saying the nanny goat had butted the patio window after seeing her reflection thinking it was another goat. She had broken the glass, so we had to return home quickly.

Gradually as the older children left to live independently, we took more children on a short-term basis. They too always accompanied us to Morfa Bychan.

We read an article in the newspaper about children from Belarus who had been badly affected by the disaster at the Chernobyl Nuclear Power Station. It had badly affected their health and bringing them to Great Britain for three weeks greatly improved their immune system. We volunteered to take one of them and were allocated an eleven-year-old girl called Dasha. She was such a polite child and it was interesting to hear about life in her country. She couldn't believe how much food we had in our shops, so different to where she lived. Organised outings were arranged for these children, horse riding, playing golf and we visited Blackpool where they could fly in a helicopter. The organisers asked carers if anyone would also like to fly in one, so I said I would love to as I had never been up in a helicopter before. We flew all over Blackpool and I loved it. We also took Dasha to stay in our caravan, which she enjoyed. When it was time for her to return home, we showered her with gifts to take with her, mainly items that were in short supply and scarce. We kept in touch with her family for many years, and I often wonder how she is now. Many of the children had short lives owing to the contamination.

One day we received a phone call about an eight-year-old little girl from Telford, and a little later her baby brother joined her. They were lovely children, but the girl was not used to dogs and was terrified every time one entered the room. She also went hysterical when one of our cats passed her. It made life very difficult. Over a period of time she improved, although she never really liked our pets.

The two children had come into care because their father had threatened to harm them if his wife didn't give him money for drugs. She was a lovely lady and when it came to the little boy's first birthday, she arrived with a tray of Indian food and fresh cream cakes. Their mother always wore very nice gold jewellery. We didn't meet the children's father, but spoke occasionally to him on the phone and I didn't like him.

The little boy took his first steps when we were on a day out on the beach at Aberaeron. The children were eventually allowed to return home, as their paternal grandmother had moved into the family home and could help to protect her grandchildren. Sadly, sometime later, we learned the father had committed suicide by jumping in front of a train.

Sometimes, as an experienced foster carer, I was asked to help at the training sessions for people applying to become foster carers. I really enjoyed them. There would be several new applicants as well as one or two professionals. On one occasion we had a psychologist and his wife who were applying to become foster carers, and at the end of the session the applicants were asked for feedback. The psychologist made a lovely comment that has stayed with me. He said, "When I grow up I want to be like Mavis."

Sometime later after he and his wife had been approved, he came back to one of our support groups as a speaker. He gave us a talk which explained how much harder it is for children who have had a difficult upbringing to deal with everyday life - something children with a stable background deal with more effectively. One of his quotes that has stayed with me was the following:

"A happy child from a stable background has an empty bucket, whereas a child from an unstable background starts with a half full bucket. Life's everyday problems are dealt with in a normal way from a child with an empty bucket, but the child whose bucket is half-full does not have capacity to deal with life's problems. He is more likely to lose his temper and kick off. So therefore, we must make allowances when looking after other people's children."

As our three long-term girls eventually left our care, we were approached to take a ten-year-old girl and her brother who was eight, long-term. They were the youngest of five children. The girl was especially good with the younger children I was looking after. I can remember one comical thing that happened when our Fostering Officer paid us a visit. Unknown to me, the girl came in the room with a cushion stuffed up her jumper and pretended to be me. It was really funny and even the fostering officer saw the funny side of it. These two children stayed with us for around eight years and even accompanied us to Tunisia when I won a "Mum in a Million" competition. A few years later we attended Tanzy's wedding. Her brother John joined the army while they were with us.

Following this, Pat and I took in a little girl aged two years. She was the next to youngest of a family of five children. Initially the three youngest went to a carer in Buckley, North Wales. As the two-year-old screamed a lot and was hard to manage, Social Services decided to separate her from her siblings. They asked if we would care for her as they thought she may have suffered brain damage as she was born prematurely.

Her speech was poor, but I immediately felt there was nothing wrong with her mentally. She improved weekly and attended nursery which helped her. They were a really close family and the social worker told me when there was only one sweet they all had a suck. I had to supervise the contact sessions between all five children. This would take place in a Social Services office in Shrewsbury. They played well together and seemed to enjoy each other's company.

She lived with us for nearly two years and the decision was made she would go for adoption. The two other young ones were going to go together, and the two eldest were going to stay in their long-term placement due to their age. I felt strongly that my little girl shouldn't be placed on her own. I sent lots of supporting letters against the decision, but it was all to no avail.

A cousin of her mother's requested she and her husband be considered. She had no children and had only ever seen the child as a tiny baby in her incubator. As family members are considered first when a child is put up for adoption, this was where she was going.

We felt extremely sad at this decision because we knew how close the children were to each other. I even pleaded and discussed with my husband to let us adopt her as we were all so fond of her, but he didn't feel it was the right thing to do at our ages.

We met the couple at the information meeting where all interested parties meet and share any information they have on the child. We didn't take to this couple and knew they were not right for her. We again voiced our opinion, but I think Social Services just thought we were saying it because we didn't want her to go. The decision for separating the children was on the recommendation of a doctor who had never met them. We commenced introductions between the little girl and her future parents. I didn't take to this couple at all, but tried hard for the sake of the child to make it work. Finally the sad day arrived when we had to take her to her new home.

When a child goes to a new family they are told to provide a welcome meal. On this occasion, however, it did not happen. We were offered a very sparse meal; the house was cold and there was a strained atmosphere. It was with a heavy heart we returned to our home having to leave her there.

Some weeks later a date was arranged for us to have contact, but it didn't happen as the adoptive mother told Social Services I had called myself Mum to the child, which was untrue and she didn't want any further contact.

I was devastated, but had to abide by her decision. I didn't hear any more of this child until some four or five years later when out of the blue, I received a message from her apologising for cancelling all contact, saying she would like us to meet again.

Apparently, she and her husband had separated because of his abusive behaviour to her, her daughter, and also her little boy she'd had two years previously. They were all residing in a women's refuge. She asked us if we could go and meet them there.

Of course, I jumped at the chance and made the necessary arrangements. It was wonderful to see this little girl, and we took her out for the afternoon. Her mum also gave me a framed photograph of her. Arrangements were then made for her to come and stay with us for an overnight visit, which she did. The child remembered the name of the girl next door to us who she had played with previously. At this time, she was around nine. After the overnight stay, we returned her to the refuge and looked forward to keeping in touch.

However, this did not happen and as mysteriously she had re-entered our lives, again, she disappeared. We heard nothing for a further two years, and I can only think that by her saying she was in regular contact with us, would help her to obtain accommodation from the council in this area as her own mum lived not too far away. I can think of no other reason.

One day I was cycling through Oswestry when lo-and-behold I saw the lady and her two children walking by the Post Office. I stopped abruptly and enquired what had happened to them. She just answered that they had had to go into hiding.

The next time we had any news of the girl was when she was sixteen years old and we were approached by Social Services to say she had run away from home and had asked if she could come back to us. Unfortunately, this was not possible as we had a houseful. Now she is an adult with two daughters of her own, and back in touch with us. I feel very sad to hear of her unhappy time growing up. She is a fantastic mother. If only they had listened to me!

It's sad that carers are not listened to more, as they know the child who has been in their care much better than anyone else. It was while I was driving this little girl to say goodbye to her birth mother that I didn't notice I was driving in a thirty-mile speed limit, because I was feeling emotional. I was listening to Cliff Richard on the radio when out stepped a policeman in the village of Hope. I burst into tears and explained why I was sad and hadn't noticed my speed, but he was unsympathetic and told me I shouldn't be driving if I was that upset. I was only driving a little over the limit. Unfortunately, I had to pay the fine. I am now very careful and watch the speedometer.

We have had both sad and happy stories during our time as carers but one very happy story illustrates how successful adoption can be. A three-week-old baby came into our care with terrible injuries, which no one was sure who had done them. She had been born to a single mother who lived in a quiet village. The baby was beautiful, but we didn't dare take her out for a few weeks in case people thought we had caused the black eye and bruises. She turned out to be a lovely, happy, smiley baby. We loved her. Everywhere we went, after her bruises had faded, people would remark how lovely she was. We became very attached to her and, of course, the old question enters, "Why can't we keep her?" Carers have to be strong and remember their job.

I can clearly remember cooking tea the night before she was going to move to her adoptive family at the age of ten months. I thought, "I have to be strong and let her move on!" Really all I wanted was to keep her. Luckily, she was moving to a family we had helped to choose, which helped a bit. We had been shown profiles of the three families short-listed and one stood out as being ideal. I remember sitting at the information meeting, and everyone was making a fuss of the new parents. They were all so happy, but nobody realised how awful I felt. It was like giving your own child away. It would have been nice to have received a bit of sympathy; we carers also have feelings. I dearly loved this child, but had to be strong in order to help other children.

As it turned out we certainly chose the right family as they told us they would keep in touch and they have. Lots of couples promise, but not many keep their word. I understand that they want to get on with caring for their new addition to the family, and don't want to think about the past. This family was certainly the exception to the rule as they told us they would keep in touch, and my word they did and still do even though she is now grown up. They informed us of her progress at school and also her musical talents. We never interfered with their lives and are still great friends.

Their daughter is now in her twenties and is successful. She plays the flute and has a very good career in local government. It is so much healthier if families are honest about adoption and this child used to tell people, "If you want a baby, just go to Mavis." She knows all about being adopted and how she lived with us and has, in fact, been to stay with us. Her new family had a daughter of ten, but had tragically lost their older son to leukaemia. The strange thing was when we visited them they brought out photographs of their son and astonishingly he was the double of the child they were adopting. I couldn't believe it. It was definitely meant to be.

Adoption is not always successful, and it is very sad when things don't work out, because the child suffers another loss. I did hear of a case where a couple had gone through all the training and introductions, but when the child was placed, the next morning the husband rang Social Services asking them to come and remove her immediately as his wife didn't want her. I am not sure what went wrong as it is unusual to return a child at that early hour. The wife probably just panicked. Sometimes training and preparation isn't as effective as it needs to be.

During our years of caring for children, we have had a few scary moments. One occasion was when we were informed that an angry mother was on the way to our home with her boyfriend to remove her baby son. We warned the police that we may need them, and I went upstairs along with a ten-year-old we were fostering and left Pat to deal with the threatening couple. He was very calm and opened the door persuading them to leave as there was no way we had the authority to give them their baby. They did leave, but we were worried they were going to damage our car. Luckily, they didn't. I certainly saw how the other half live, and the chaos of some of their lives.

Children born into a loving, stable family have an advantage over those who don't have supportive parents or those who have no structure in their lives. Time and time again we have looked after children who have lived traumatic lives. Women get into relationships with unsavoury characters, sometimes having children with them, and those relationships affect the children.

Children deserve better. When they move to secure placements and have a regular routine, they thrive. It's not money that's important, but love and stability. It's also important that children learn right from wrong. They should know the boundaries. Some parents let children do what they want and don't like to say no. I think they should learn respect and how to behave. I do not understand parents who let their children go to bed when they like. I believe in routine and certain rules.

In 2003, we were asked to go to Shrewsbury to collect a six-month-old baby girl who was being cared for by her grandmother. Her mother was involved with drugs. We were told the child was suffering from eczema as her skin was covered in blotchy sores and the Health Visitor agreed.

However, we soon began to itch as well, and it became unbearable. We couldn't stop scratching. We even took a fork to bed so we could scratch ourselves! Our doctor said we were suffering from scabies. With the help of medication, it soon cleared.

The little girl, who was such a pretty baby, didn't return to her mother, but was adopted by her father's brother and his partner. Unfortunately, their relationship broke down as he had an affair with an eighteen-year-old. The partner kept the child and has now married. Every Christmas we receive a photograph of her. She is now fifteen years old and is still very pretty.

When new parents are chosen for a child, I can't help feeling jealous. I feel as though the child is mine, especially if I have had them directly from hospital. However, carers have to remember that it is a temporary situation. Usually it isn't long before another placement arrives and I move on, but it can still be very emotional. Even with training, those feelings are normal. As I said earlier we, as carers, have to attend training courses, some mandatory, but others are optional. It is always nice to meet other carers, and it is good to widen our knowledge base. Anything a carer can learn is useful while doing this difficult job.

One of our more difficult placements was a five-year-old boy whose family lived on a narrow boat. He had an unhealthy fascination for cars, and had tried to start his parents' car. As soon as he arrived at our house, he shot up our stairs and opened all the bedroom windows. We had to hide the car keys and keep the windows locked shut. It was quite scary as we weren't sure what he was capable of doing. We definitely had to keep a careful watch over him. Luckily he didn't stay with us for long, before moving to a long-term carer in Shrewsbury. I sometimes wonder what became of him.

Another little boy arrived who was autistic. He was four years old and very sweet. He was being cared for by his granny. His fascination was doors. He opened and shut them constantly, running from room to room. After a while with us, he moved back in with his grandmother.

The next child was a lovely twelve-month-old. Her father was a paedophile and his partner was supposed to keep a watch over her, and not to leave her on her own with him. However, it came to light that he had been out alone with her in the car, so she was removed. The father wasn't very pleasant and dictated which nappies I was to use. He refused point blank to allow her to have the MMR jab. The baby's mum was a pretty girl, but very quiet and completely under his control.

We loved this child. She had large eyes and reminded me of a doll. The mum became pregnant with her second baby so I agreed to take this one as well when it was born. I can clearly remember attending a meeting and all the mum could say was, *"Oh, it's nice she will be joining her sister."* She wasn't at all upset that she would soon be losing another child. The new baby arrived, and we went to the Maternity ward to collect her. Something didn't seem right with the baby as she was too quiet. She just wasn't thriving.

The Health Visitor didn't show any concern, but I was worried. One evening in the early hours the baby was finding it hard to breathe, so I rang ShropDoc, the NHS emergency service. Breaking all speed limits, we drove to Shrewsbury on their advice. The doctor said I should dilute her feeds. He told me I would be okay with my experience, but I still wasn't happy and didn't follow his instructions.

However, things got worse and as I had to take her to a consultant at the Orthopaedic Hospital about another matter, I voiced my concerns. He immediately told me I was to take her to The Royal Shrewsbury Hospital Neo-Natal Unit. I did so and straight away there were several medical staff around her.

It was touch and go as the baby fought to survive. Diluting her formula in this case was the wrong thing to do. It was a relief to hear that, because although I always trust my instinct, you do sometimes wonder whether it is right.

She was put on oxygen and I sat by her cot all day. At night, as I lay in bed, I dreaded the phone ringing. Luckily, she improved. They diagnosed her with bronchiolitis which affects the lungs. After two weeks in hospital, she returned to us, but it was the most frightening experience and one I will never forget. It's always more frightening when a child who isn't mine becomes ill.

The sisters had regular contact with their parents. On one occasion we were on holiday and it was arranged we would meet them in Betwys-y-Coed. It turned out to be a very sunny, hot day. The mum was more interested in keeping out of the sun than communicating with her children.

At the age of four and sixteen months, they were adopted by two teachers who we liked. We have visited them twice and they are thriving. They have moved away from the area now, but went on to adopt two more children. Every Christmas we receive a lovely letter and photograph of all four children. Such a happy ending!

We soon had another little girl brought around by a social worker. She was thirteen-months-old. Her mother was British and her father was from a country on the other side of the world.

I went outside to meet them. The child had big, brown eyes, olive skin, and was exceptionally pretty. She looked at me and gave a huge smile, which melted my heart. They both came in and we filled in the necessary paperwork. The social worker left and the little girl settled immediately by walking around holding the furniture. It wasn't long before she learned to walk independently. We fell in love with her straight away. She was feisty and full of character. Unfortunately, we had a difficult relationship with her mother and I think she resented us caring for her child, which I suppose is understandable. On several occasions she told lies about us on contact visits. I felt as though she was trying to get us into trouble.

She once told Social Services that the child's clothes were dirty which was upsetting, particularly as the little girl had arrived in very scruffy clothing that was too small.

Carers have to detach from the situation and try to be understanding. After twelve months with us, the decision was made that the girl wouldn't return to the care of her mother. Her paternal grandparents applied to have her, and after a visit by the social worker to their far-off country they were approved. Arrangements were made for them to travel to Britain for the introductions to take place. As the social worker was going to be on holiday, we supervised all the contacts.

First, we took her to the Wynnstay Hotel in town, which is where her grandparents were staying. Although she had never seen them before she loved all the attention she received and we also liked them. On future visits, she would become excited when we neared the hotel. We took them around the area which I think they appreciated. They also came to our house for a dinner of roast beef and Yorkshire pudding, which we felt was a typical British meal. On the Sunday before returning home they attended a Sunday morning service at our church in full national costume.

We set off early the following day to drive to Heathrow airport, stopping for a meal at the services on the motorway. We said our goodbyes at the airport and that was the last we saw of her. Afterward, we received a couple of emails informing us she was okay and learning their language.

We didn't hear anything more and hope the year spent with us gave her stability and that she was able to transfer her attachment to her new family. We have so many happy memories of this lovely little girl.

Two weeks after she left we were asleep in bed when the phone rang in the early hours of the morning. Sleepily I lifted the receiver to hear a social worker saying, "You have a vacancy, haven't you?"

When I said we had, he replied, "Can you go to Shrewsbury Police Station and collect an eleven-month-old little girl. She has been removed from her home due to a disturbance." We later learnt her parents were on drugs, and spent their days walking the streets.

We quickly threw some clothes on and soon were on our way to Shrewsbury. We certainly saw another life at the Police Station with people being brought in and held in custody. It felt a little strange sitting there amongst all the activity.

We then met this adorable child who was in the arms of a Policeman. She gave me a big smile and I went to change her nappy in the ladies' toilets. She was suffering from terrible nappy rash. After the formalities were completed, we drove home where we placed her straight into a cot and she promptly fell asleep until morning.

She had regular contact with her mother and grandmother, but limited contact with her father. She had spent the majority of her life in a buggy, and had no idea how to stand on her legs. She would just sit down when we tried to stand her up.

We had planned to go on holiday just after she arrived, so she accompanied us to Anglesey where we had booked a plot on a site. She really enjoyed staying in our caravan and in a short while learned to stand on her legs. Everyone loved her. She learned to walk at the age of fourteen months. Things seemed to be progressing well enough for her to return home to the care of her mother who was very likeable, but, as often happens, things began to deteriorate and her mother hadn't been able to quit her use of drugs. So it was decided against her going home.

Her Mum's sister offered to care for her. She already had a lively four-year-old little boy, was pregnant, and due to give birth in a couple of months. I was a little worried as to whether this was the ideal placement.

One day the child was having contact with her Aunty preparing her for moving in when a solicitor started pushing for her to go there and then. The first indication that she wouldn't be returning to us was when the social worker rang. We were extremely upset as we hadn't said goodbye or had time to prepare ourselves or the child for her departure.

On hindsight, I think we should have done more to prevent the sudden move. This is not how it should be done nor is it how it usually happens. The Aunty did keep in touch for a while and we did meet up once. The little girl looked well cared for and happy, but sadly it didn't work out. I was very upset when I learned the child was back in the care system and had been moved to another carer. We already had placements, so they didn't ask us which was such a shame. It was a pity because the little girl was two years older than if she had moved earlier to an adoptive home. The younger children are, the better they settle. I did meet up with her new carer at a function and arranged to go and see her, but unfortunately, before I did, she was moved to another family. I just hope she is thriving.

While a child is in care, we keep a memory book, which keeps a record of any events in a child's life. This accompanies them wherever they move to as it helps the child understand things more clearly and fills in the gaps in their life which can so easily get lost.

At the same time, we were caring for this child, we were returning from one of our breaks in our touring caravan when we received a request to take at short notice a five-month-old baby girl. There had been a domestic at her home where the boyfriend had attacked the baby's mother. It was unusual for us to have two little ones from separate families at the same time, but Social Services must have been pretty desperate to find someone with a vacancy with it being the holiday period. A gorgeous little baby arrived quite late in the evening. All she ever did was smile, and it certainly helped that both children were content.

Contact between two sets of parents and attending all the necessary meetings was time-consuming. Looking after the children was the easy part, but at that time support workers were in short supply, so we kept getting requests to drive the children to their different contacts, which was often difficult. Life became extremely hectic, but I loved it.

After a couple of months, however, the baby moved with her mum to a mother and baby placement. After being there for some time, they moved back to the area they originally came from down south. It was certainly easier just having one child again!

A few years later we met up with baby's birth father who had since fathered another child with a different partner. This child had also come into care. What a mess!

After the little girl who went to her Aunty had moved, we were quiet for some time, but then received a request to take a newborn girl who again had been born in Shrewsbury Maternity Hospital. The little girl was the third child to be born to a woman who had been responsible, together with her partner, for horrific abuse against her first born when he was five years old. We weren't aware at the time that years before, the women's partner had been responsible for the death of a child from a previous partner, while they lived in a different part of the country.

The five-year-old had been starved, beaten and teased. He used to pinch other children's packed lunches at school because he was so hungry. The mother denied being responsible and may not have been the abuser. We will never know, but she didn't protect him from this vile man.

Apparently, they would play a ball game and if he dropped the ball, he would be smacked. Other horrible things took place. He eventually moved on to be adopted. Because of this, the next child was moved at birth and adopted. This third pregnancy was the result of a drunken liaison with a man at a party.

I remember meeting the mother soon after the baby had been placed with us. She lived in fantasy land and didn't have a clue about being a mother. She held the baby in one arm and her bottle in the other. The baby made it obvious that she was hungry, but all she did was wave the bottle over the baby's head until I couldn't stand it any longer and had to intervene. She would constantly talk to the baby as though it was an adult and understood what she was saying. I think this was more for my benefit than for her baby.

Social Services gave her every opportunity to get her baby back and even spent a vast amount of money on a special therapy course. I was adamant the baby should not return to her care. Poor little thing made it clear with her eyes that she didn't enjoy being in her mother's company. She was always so happy when she returned to us.

When I handed the child to her mother, she would look at me as if to say, "Please don't leave me with her." Eventually - thank goodness - the court decided, along with the therapy company, that she shouldn't be returned to her mother.

When the baby was eight months old Social Services contacted the man who it was thought was the father, and after verification by DNA, they asked if he wanted to be considered as a carer for his child.

His first introduction to her was when we met at a venue in Oswestry, and I was immediately impressed with how he reacted. He was a lovely lad and did all the right things. He was very honest and stated that he didn't have a lot of experience in caring for children, but was willing to learn. He was close to his sister who had two boys, and she helped him a lot. He didn't have a home of his own, but was intending to find a house to rent.

During the next few weeks, he learned how to be a good dad and clearly loved his daughter. It was decided the little girl, who was now around thirteen months old, should move to the care of her father. We couldn't have been happier. He found a house to rent not far from his sister and her family and turned it into a real home. We were invited to her second birthday party. He turned out to be a competent father. It's mind-boggling to think he hadn't been aware he had a child a few months previously. We are still in touch with them.

Foster carers have to attend the mandatory training courses and there are numerous voluntary courses as well. It is nice to mix with other carers. Once a month most areas hold a monthly forum, which is quite informal. We usually went to the one held at The Railway Pub in Yorton, near Shawbury. Occasionally there would be a speaker or we would chat discussing any problems we may have. Sandwiches and pickles were also provided. It was always an enjoyable evening out.

During our years of caring we hardly ever requested respite as we felt that the children were part of the family and should accompany us, where possible, on holidays. The only time we needed it was during our trips to London to see the musicals because the coach would leave at six o'clock in the morning and didn't return home until around ten o'clock at night.

We had no alternative, but we did find the decision ridiculous not to let our friends, who were CRB checked and their home approved, care for our baby overnight. The baby knew our friends and was happy in their company, but instead had to go and stop with a carer who he had never met. I suppose rules are rules, but it didn't make sense.

Another of the children who arrived at our house was a newborn baby boy, who was the second child born to a single mum. She had had a daughter the previous year that had moved on to adoption. She was living with the father of her first child but had found herself pregnant when he was serving a prison sentence, after a brief affair with her mother's boyfriend. She was a likeable girl and when her boyfriend was discharged from prison, he stood by her and said he wanted to parent this little boy.

At the baby's six week check it was noticed that his head measured larger than average, so may have been suffering from hydrocephalus. We had to take him to the orthopaedic hospital for a check-up. They decided he needed an MRI scan, and this had to take place at Birmingham Children's Hospital and would take all day.

We arrived at the ward early in the morning and were shown his bed. As he was an extremely active little boy, it proved quite difficult to keep him from falling off it. We gave him his sedative and accompanied him to where the large scanner was. At this point, he was fast asleep, but as soon as the machine fired up it sounded like a steam train entering a tunnel, and he woke up screaming. The nurse wasn't too happy and said, "We can't carry on as he has to be still. You will have to return tomorrow and we'll try again."

"Please try once more" I asked, as I didn't fancy another long day. We rocked him back to sleep and luckily with the help of ear plugs managed to get it done. What a relief! We later learned that they couldn't find anything wrong with him.

The boy became quite a handful as he grew older, managing to open cupboards and we even had to remove the knob from the fridge.

He was never still. He had a huge appetite and there was nothing that he wouldn't eat. We had to put him on solid food earlier than usual to satisfy his hunger.

He had regular contact with his mother and limited contact with her boyfriend. It reached the stage where he was spending all day with the two of them in their flat. However, things suddenly took a turn for the worse just before he was due to return to them permanently. There was an incident at the flat involving a broken front door. I am not entirely sure what happened, but contact was stopped immediately.

Around this time, we learnt that his mother was pregnant again. The decision was made to have him adopted and Social Services approached the couple who had already adopted his older sister. They decided they would like to have him as well.

Siblings are offered to couples who have adopted older brothers or sisters. The prospective parents were a very quiet couple who clearly loved their daughter, but I wondered if they realised what was about to descend on them. They lived in a small house, so it was already crowded. I was a little worried as to whether he would be okay. As I left him he looked anxiously at us and the social worker later told me when anyone else came to the house he would stare at the door. We delayed visiting him for three months to give him time to forget us. We then met up with him and his family at a play area and thank goodness he had forgotten us. He looked very happy with his new family although he still was pulling his sister's hair.

Over the years, we have made some lovely fostering friends with whom we stay in contact. Foster carers now receive training before they are approved, and this is ongoing. In the days we were approved, no training was available initially, but later on we attended all the courses that we could. A carer can never know it all. I did my NVQ level 3, and we both completed The Standards.

People may think that carers don't need training if they have brought up their own children, but looking after other people's children with complex needs is very different. Carers are always learning and each child looked after is different. Techniques that may work with one child, may not work with another. The role of a caregiver is the most rewarding role to play in the life of a child, and all of the hurdles and trials are well worth it.

Support Worker

One day, I noticed an advert in the newspaper by Shropshire County Council advertising for Family Support Workers on a part-time basis. I applied and was successful. This worked well with our role of foster carers. It involved helping to support families who were struggling, and also involved transporting children to contact dates with their families. Sometimes I had to supervise these contacts. I loved this work and didn't half see life as I came into contact with a wide range of families.

One family was more entertaining than a soap opera. The mother would shout, "Bloody stop swearing," to her four-year-old son. I also fostered him, and he swore like a trooper. We once took him to see a children's film and in a loud voice, he shouted a big swear word at the screen.

It can be embarrassing when you can't explain that he isn't yours. I worked with the family for over a year and could have written another book on all the things I saw and heard!

On another occasion, we took an eleven-year-old girl and her six-year-old brother into our family. They had lost their mother and the girl was very upset and she cried a lot. Looking back, I think she probably needed counselling. In between crying sessions, she would sing along to the radio, and now when I hear the song, "Brown Girl In The Ring," it reminds me of her.

After a year with us they moved to a long-term placement, but unfortunately the carer made inappropriate advances to another girl they were looking after, and so all children were moved. These two children eventually went to live with a relative. She regularly wrote to me after they had moved and visited us on numerous occasions with her family.

One Boxing Day evening, many years ago, we received a knock on the door. A six-foot, twenty five year old man was standing there. It was her brother. He still keeps in touch and has even been here for a meal with his wife. He goes under another name now as he was a witness in a murder case and had to move to another area. His sister is now a grandmother.

In my role as Family Support Worker, I was introduced to a family with an eight-year-old who, it was said, was out of control. I must admit this was the most difficult and worrying of the children I had come across.

As we travelled in my car, he terrorised my little dog and if she could have spoken I think she would have told me how frightened of him she was, as when I wasn't watching he was nasty to her.

After working with him we fostered him for a short time and one day, while talking to someone in the lounge, the other children informed me he had swung one of our cats around by the tail. He certainly had a sadistic streak.

One thing he loved doing was barricading frogs in compounds so that they couldn't escape. As with all our children, we took him to the caravan. One day we went out for a short while, leaving our poodle in the caravan. He had been out playing, but had returned while we were away. When we got back our little dog was shivering in fear. He then moved to some friends of ours on a more permanent placement. We warned them what he was capable of and they took great care to watch him. Unfortunately, he shut the door as their spaniel was going out and almost killed her. I often wonder what became of him and just hope he hasn't harmed anyone.

I had met Mary, and her husband Garry, at one of our foster support groups – they have since become firm friends. She told me she initially thought I lived on a farm, as I was always talking about our animals. We have continued our friendship even though we have now both finished fostering.

We had another little girl aged about seven who we certainly had to watch with our dogs. I had been working with her family as a support worker and she was the middle child with two brothers. They lived with their mum and stepdad. I was frightened of the stepdad, as he was not very friendly.

To keep the children out of his way the mother and three children would all be in their nightwear before he returned from work at tea time, and would go to bed early.

She was eventually given the choice of staying with her husband and losing her children, or leaving him and keeping her children. I couldn't believe she chose her husband.

Their daughter came to stay with us, the elder boy stayed with a relative, and the younger one moved in with other carers, eventually moving to an adoptive placement.

The girl could be very cruel to our dogs and she was quite clever at doing it when we weren't looking and denying it when confronted. Eventually, she too moved to an adoptive placement, but this broke down and she then lived in a care home. She did keep in touch. She continued to be a member of the Girls Brigade which she had attended while living with us.

I still hear from her from time to time and apparently she is doing well. She fondly remembers her time spent with us. Such good news that she is doing well, despite her terrible start in life.

Another interesting case was when we were asked to take a twelve-year-old boy. His father had hit him over the head with a spade while digging the garden. He could easily have killed him. The case went to court and although all through it his mother stuck by her husband -after he was found guilty, the marriage eventually broke down and the couple divorced. I wondered if the husband could be the Yorkshire ripper, who at that time was murdering women around Leeds and Manchester. I rang the Yorkshire Police, but of course he wasn't.

This young lad was very intelligent and Social Services paid for him to attend boarding school. I often wonder what he is doing now. He could be a professor somewhere, perhaps? I remember the time he got us into trouble by climbing on the toilet roof of the caravan site, which was very embarrassing. It would have been very tempting to say, "He isn't ours." He was our responsibility and we could not do that.

As I have said being a support worker worked well alongside being a foster carer. Another family I worked with lived in a top floor of a terraced house. They had two or three large dogs in a very small flat, which was a bit untidy and dark. It was certainly an eye opener to see how other people lived.

On another occasion, we were asked to accommodate two little boys aged two and three years. They had a younger brother and lived with their mum and her boyfriend. The youngest brother was in his cot when he sustained an injury and had a nasty wound on his head. Hence the boys were removed from the home and the baby taken to hospital. The police came to interview them, but owing to their young age, they didn't find out who was responsible for the attack. I don't think anyone was charged with the assault.

The baby was so badly injured he had brain damage and eventually confined to a wheelchair. He went to live with his grandmother.

Around nine years later one of the brothers who had come to us called at our house and said, "I used to live with you."

I don't know who had told him, as he would have been too young to remember, but it is always nice when children come and visit.

Sometimes life doesn't always work out for these youngsters- one day we were reading the local paper when we read about a boy we had cared for, who, along with a friend, was responsible for breaking into the bungalow of an elderly man. They attacked him and the man later died of his injuries. Both boys were found guilty of murder and are serving life sentences in prison.

One of my assignments as a support worker was to travel to Penrith in Cumbria to collect an eleven-year-old boy, who was attending a residential school there. I was to bring him back to stay in this area so he could have contact with his family. I had also been working with another child in his family. Pat drove me and after a very long journey we picked him up and drove him back to the carers who would be looking after him during his visit. We were both very tired as it had been a long day, but when we drew up outside their house, he flatly refused to get out of the car. Nothing would persuade him to enter their home. After some time and threatening to leave him outside, he eventually relented. What a relief!

On another occasion, I had to take a six-year-old for contact with her elderly father. He lived in a small, scruffy terraced cottage. He obviously loved his little girl, but having convictions of child abuse he could not be left alone with her. This child was moved later to an adoptive placement. I have learned so much by working with all sorts of families.

Mum in a Million

During the children's six-week school summer holiday we had gone to our caravan near Aberystwyth. I received a phone call from the local paper informing me I was the local winner of a competition being run nationwide by The Hospital Savings Association to find a Mum in a Million.

Apparently, Emma who was then twenty-four years old had written a letter nominating me. She mentioned many lovely things, including me being a foster carer and how living with us had changed her life. This is her letter:

Mavis Humby is my foster mum and been a foster mum to about 80 other children, including bringing up two of her own over the past 24 years.

I first met her when I was 5. My younger sister, Jenny was aged 3, and we had been split up from our older sister, Julie, 6, and Mavis was fostering her.

Social Services were desperately trying to find a family to foster all three of us together as Jenny and I were being moved around a lot.

As you can imagine, it was very confusing for us at that age. We couldn't believe it when our social worker told us that Mavis and her husband Patrick had agreed to foster us and we were going to live with Julie.

Since then, Mavis has been my mum and the best that I could have hoped for. She struggled to make sure we were happy and had everything we needed even when that meant going without things herself.

I left home at 20, but she is still my mum and she is always there if I need help or advice.

Jenny left home at 18 and became pregnant. Mum was very shocked and upset but was still there for her and helped her get back on her feet. Now she adores Jenny's daughter, Jessica, but doesn't like being called Nanny because she thinks it makes her sound old!

Apart from me and my sisters, (which were enough to cope with), I've already said she's fostered around 80 children and is still fostering now. At the moment, she has Tanzy, aged 13, her brother, John, aged 11, and Rosie, aged 4. She is very proud of the fact that at the age of 55 she rides her bike many times a day with Rosie on the back!

Some foster children have been difficult to cope with. One even shot next door's cat with a bow and arrow, and guess who had to take it round to give them the bad new and apologise – yes Mavis did!

She loves animals and has taken in many a distressed pet and found them homes, which has driven poor Dad mad at times.

As well as fostering, she is a member of Christchurch and used to be secretary for the newsletter she did extremely well with Christian Aid envelopes, this year and she'll always help out if she can with church activities. She also finds time to go to WI (Women's Institute). She has a part time job with Social Services as a Family Support Worker and visits young mothers to give them help where they may need it. She has also done training courses so that she can train new foster parents.

When her father died about five years ago, her mother was diagnosed as having Alzheimer's disease. There was no way Mum was having her put into a home so she took her in and cared for her, which was tremendous, both physically and mentally, until her mum died a few years later.

I went to see Mum the other day, and we had a good chat about a few things. She was a bit down, which is very unusual for her. She'd had to make a heart-breaking decision about little Rosie's future.

One of the things she said really made me think. She said she wished she could have a lovely relaxing holiday abroad, and that it wasn't fair that lots of people she knew were jetting off abroad, and she couldn't afford it. Although she loves her time in their caravan, it would be nice to 'get away from it all.'

I thought if I had the money I would pay for them to go as I feel I can't repay her enough for all the things she's done for me. Then I saw the advert in the Oswestry Advertizer for a 'Mum in a Million' competition.

What a great way to give her, and her husband, Pat, of course, the recognition she deserves and the holiday she always wanted.

After all she'd done for other people, it is about time she was given something in return, and she is definitely a Mum in a Million!

The prize for winning the first round was a weekend for two in a Jarvis Hotel of our choice. I was so excited, but was still a bit down that a little girl we were fostering would be leaving our family in the coming weeks.

On returning home from the caravan we made the necessary arrangements for the children and our pets to be looked after and headed off to the Jarvis Hotel in York. We had a lovely weekend exploring the city and enjoying being looked after for a change.

To my utter surprise, I got through to another round and the prize was a meal for Pat and me, plus two others, which meant we could take Emma, who had nominated me, and my daughter, Lisa. We chose to

MUM IN A MILLION
H
H S A
A

Congratulations

to

Mavis Humby

as a

REGIONAL WINNER

in the

HSA MUM IN A MILLION
CAMPAIGN 1995

James Lyon

have it at The Sweeney Hotel. A representative from the HSA and his wife also came. Winning a further round meant Pat and I, plus our two foster children, went to stay in a log cabin on a lovely leisure park in Siloth in Cumbria. We had a great time there.

The final prize was a week in Tunisia for four people. All the finalists were invited on a mini cruise to Spain on the ship named The Pride of Bilbao, where the winner would be announced.

We would spend three nights on the ship, which was huge. Pat and I had planned to spend another two nights away after the mini cruise had finished.

The two of us boarded the ship on Saturday evening, leaving our car in a parking bay reserved for passengers. We had a lovely cabin and then gathered to be welcomed by representatives from the HSA. They told us we were all invited on Saturday evening to the ship's theatre, which held three thousand people.

Pat and I made friends with another couple. All the finalists gathered together when later in the evening to my absolute astonishment, I was announced as the overall winner!

There had been 34,000 entries originally and around two hundred of these were eligible to go on the cruise. I was made to feel like Miss World with cameras everywhere. I had to do a short speech and as the day before I had been feeling a little seasick, my first words were, "Oh, I am glad I don't feel sick." It was probably not the way to start, but the audience laughed.

Next morning, I was filmed giving an interview with a representative from the HSA. We then had to assemble in the ship's cinema where the Minister of Transport gave a speech all in Spanish and I was filmed by Spanish television. We then moved to the outer deck, and I was introduced to the Spanish Minister and he gave me a kiss. Unfortunately, he didn't speak a word of English.

While moored in Bilbao we were taken on a coach trip around the area. It was all a very memorable experience and I enjoyed my moment of fame. Unfortunately, we were on our way to collect our car and had boarded a coach to take us to the car park area, but no one would let us sit on the lower floor so we had to climb upstairs.

Although I was the outright winner, not everyone was pleased. Some of the husbands felt that their wives should have won. As mentioned before we had planned to extend our holiday by a few days, but I couldn't wait to return home to share my good news as we were both so excited.

Next morning, I hadn't yet come down to earth when the phone rang and it was Radio Shropshire, who interviewed me live on air.

The press had a field day and it wasn't long before Pat, Emma and I travelled to London to appear on ITV's breakfast show. We travelled by train, were met at the station, and transported to a lovely hotel in Drury Lane. Next morning, there was Emma and I sitting in the Green Room - only it isn't green, waiting to be interviewed by the presenter known as 'Beechie'. I can remember seeing myself on the monitor. As we finished the interview, a lady who looked familiar said to me, "Oh, I know you," but I think she had mixed me up with someone else. It turned out to be Sally Thomsett from the Railway Children and Man about the House. Wow!

The local newspaper then wanted to do a story with photographs, and just as we thought we were returning to normal we received a call from Channel 5 to ask us if they could come and do a short film.

The day arrived and a presenter, a cameraman, and numerous others invaded our home. They rearranged furniture, ornaments and pictures. I felt very self-conscious when being filmed. We weren't allowed to include any of the children in our care, only Emma, because of confidentiality. Emma was old enough to give her consent. Unfortunately, a camera was damaged while filming, worth thousands of pounds and everything had to come to a standstill while a replacement arrived from London. They spent three days at our home, but when it appeared on television it was on for only a matter of minutes. Goodness only knows how long it takes to film something any longer.

After appearing on television and with all the publicity people would stop us in the street saying they had seen us on the television. We also had a write up in TV Times, but I'm afraid some old photos of children were published, and Social Services took a dim view because identification of children in care is prohibited.

We doubted very much anyone would be able to identify them as they were from years ago. However, the adoptive mum of the little girl I spoke about earlier saw it as an opportunity to have some compensation, and sent a solicitor's letter trying to claim her child had been badly affected. Luckily our solicitor replied that the child was old enough to know she had lived with us and been adopted, so nothing more was done.

Gradually things died down, and we were forgiven. The following February we spent one week in Tunisia with two of our children, which we enjoyed very much. Apart from one holiday in our teens some thirty-two years ago, we hadn't been abroad or been on a large aeroplane. The only time we had set foot on a plane was on a pleasure flight in Blackpool, and in a two-sitter plane owned by a friend of Pat's in Oswestry.

The first thing that hit us as we stepped off the plane was the warm air, but as it was their winter, being February, the locals were all wearing anoraks whereas we were in t-shirts. The hotel was gorgeous, and we all enjoyed ourselves, although one of the local men wanted to buy our fourteen-year-old! I shall always be grateful to Emma for entering me in that competition.

Royal Garden Party

One day I was accompanying a friend at court in Telford regarding the adoption of her two children when my mobile rang. It was Pat ringing from his office in Birmingham to ask if I would like to go to London, as we were to have an invitation to meet the Queen.

It appeared the Lord Chancellor's department always check in advance in case anybody turns down the invitation. Also, apparently, the Chairman of Severn Trent Water Authority, Pat`s employers, decided to offer us the invitation to attend a garden party at Buckingham Palace, after hearing about our work over the past twenty years fostering.

We were so excited, and I bought a posh dress and hat. My friend Mary decorated my hat with the same material of the dress, and I wore high heels. Lisa and her husband came to London with us, but not into the Palace. We stayed overnight in a very nice hotel. I can remember how we took photos of each other in all our finery before we left the hotel.

Lisa dropped us outside the Palace and it was hard to believe we were actually going inside - as this was at a time when no members of the public were allowed.

An ex-lord mayor of London, who was standing next to us, explained the procedure and escorted us through the gates of the Palace and into the grounds.

On many occasions, I had peered through the railings wondering what it was like inside. Those attending formed a queue until an official beckoned us forward. We entered through one of the entrances and into a long corridor where I noticed a pigeon sitting on eggs. Buckingham Palace is huge, bigger than I had imagined. We walked through where I had seen royalty on television coming out of glass doors and eventually reached a large room where I sat on a huge settee. I had to pinch myself that I wasn't dreaming and yes, I was actually sitting inside Buckingham Palace.

We then went outside through large double doors, down some steps, and onto the lawns at the rear. The crowd mingled with each other and we met some interesting people from all walks of life. We ate afternoon tea with cakes, cucumber sandwiches, and iced tea. Pat and I looked into the summerhouse where there were little bowls of water for the royal corgis. We walked down to the beautiful lake where there were flamingos.

The only people who met the Queen were the ones previously chosen to do so, but we did get quite near. I was surprised as to how small Queen Elizabeth was. She was swinging an umbrella. It certainly was an amazing experience, even if my feet were killing me from walking around in high heels.

More Placements

Although we have cared for every age of child, I particularly enjoyed the newborn babies. As I became older, decided that this was the age I wanted to concentrate on. One such baby was particularly tiny and was the smallest we'd had. She weighed just five pounds. The nurse showed her to us and just said, "Can you dress her?" and then left us to it. I was all fingers and thumbs, but managed to do so. It was a bit scary with her being so tiny.

However as soon as I arrived home, I gained my confidence. We thought she was small, but little did we know that a few years later we would look after a much smaller baby. I firmly believe that even newborns love cuddles and respond to conversation. We moved her on to an adoptive family and many more babies followed.

One year, just before Easter, we arranged to pick up a baby girl from the maternity unit at the Orthopaedic Hospital. As we were about to go on holiday, we took her with us. She was adopted by two doctors and we never saw her again. Another baby we collected was a six-pound baby boy from the Maternity ward at the Royal Shrewsbury Hospital. His mother had had a little girl, two years previously who had been adopted. She had actually spent all her maternity grant on her baby, which doesn't always happen. He came with pram, cot, clothes, nappies and cuddly toys. I am sure she loved her children, it was her lifestyle preventing her from caring for them, which was sad.

As we were leaving I said to her, "Aren't you going to give him a kiss?" So, she did. She then phoned me regularly to check on his progress and had regular contact, missing only a few meetings.

The baby's grandparents also visited him. As she wasn't sure who the baby's father was, we had to take the baby for a DNA test. At the age of eight months, it was decided he should join his sister, and the family still keeps in touch. He is now ten years old. It is lovely to hear how he is doing. I find it rewarding when children move to a better life and we like to think the time spent with us helps them, even if they don't remember it.

He moved in the August and in the September we were put on hold to take a baby that was due any day. The father had a history of sexual abuse against children and his partner had learning difficulties. She also didn't have any maternal instinct.

When we receive a request to take a baby, I get excited and on this occasion, I was in the hairdressers in Trefonen when I heard a baby boy had been born, a healthy eight pounds. We arranged to go and collect him the next day. He was lovely, although he was suffering from a sore bottom. I can't understand how this happened, but maybe his mother hadn't changed him as often as she should, and nobody had noticed. He came with very few possessions, unlike the previous baby. We soon grew to love him. His mother and father lived together, but his mother had no interest in being a parent although they had regular contact. As he grew older, he became fond of cars and learned to recognise the different makes.

All Landrover Discoveries were Pat's cars and all small Peugeot's were Memie's cars. He grew very close to the both of us and it is a shame, but for different reasons his future kept being deferred in court. By the time a final decision was made for him to be adopted, he was two and a half years old. We dreaded him moving. Finally, a couple were chosen who already had an older son, and we liked them. Even so, it was extremely hard to let him go, and we were both very upset. Luckily, they keep in touch and regularly send us photographs. Apparently, he still loves cars and has been to see Formula One racing at Silverstone and has visited

Disneyland in Florida. What a lucky boy, and what a lucky couple to have found such a lovely little lad.

Two lovely children, a girl aged three and her two-year-old brother came to stay with us. They were from a small town some miles away. The girl was very streetwise and had certainly seen life. She was a real chatterbox. After a year with us she returned home, but her brother stayed with us for a further year. I also visited their family as a support worker. Their mother went on to have two further children.

On one occasion, I had taken the little boy to a local beauty spot, and as he was playing in the shallow stream he fell under the water. I rushed over and was able to grab him. It turned out the water went deep in one part. I had to be prepared for quick action with all of our little ones.

The question people often ask us is, "Don't you miss them when they move on?" The answer is yes, we do.

If the children had not moved on, then we couldn't care for the ones that need our help. We just hope we have helped them during this difficult period in their lives and on occasions it can be a relief when they move on, especially if they have been really difficult. They are my children while they are with us, but as soon as I know they are moving on or when their new family is chosen, I know they are not mine anymore.

Of course, it has become easier as I have grown older, but it can still be very hard. All children who have to leave their families are affected in some way, some more than others. It can be very worrying when some settle too well, but we try and show them love and respect during the time they are with us. All children respond to love. Kathleen once gave me good advice, which I have never forgotten:

"You may not love them all, but always try to be fair."

Celebrations and Clubs

When I celebrated my fiftieth birthday, I was told we were meeting the family for a meal, and we drove out of Oswestry, parking by the canal at Ellesmere. I wondered why we had stopped there, but Pat said he wanted to see a colleague who was staying on a canal narrow boat. He asked me to accompany him and although I didn't really want to, I agreed.

We arrived at a large, narrow boat and to my absolute astonishment, all of my family and friends began cheering as I entered. They had all been invited to join in my birthday celebrations. It truly was a wonderful surprise, and usually I don't like surprises, but this was lovely and all arranged by Lisa, my wonderful daughter, assisted by my equally wonderful husband!

For my 51st birthday, Lisa and Nick bought me tickets to see Joseph and his Technicolour Dreamcoat in London, and we stayed overnight. This happened a few days after we had moved one of our babies, so it certainly cheered me up. Unfortunately, while I was there I received a phone call to say Mum had died. She was in respite care whilst we were away.

I also enjoyed a lovely sixtieth birthday, as Pat and I went to Manchester to see Phantom of the Opera, and stayed overnight in a hotel.

For the next milestone, I wondered what they had arranged for my seventieth in 2010, but was assured this was going to be immediate family coming to a meal at The Sweeney Hotel. I should have guessed, but I didn't, even when I noticed a couple who were our friends in the bar. As I entered the restaurant everyone started cheering. I then realised it was for me. All our family and friends were there; sadly the only people missing were Kathleen and Keith.

We were looking after a toddler at the time, so I also had him with me. The first thing I said was, "Who is paying for all this?" It was another lovely surprise, and we had a lovely meal.

We arranged another party the following July for Pat's seventieth. This time it was a hog roast at Oswestry Cricket Club and we had another lovely reunion, again with our family and friends, although this time it wasn't a surprise. I can't believe we are both now well into our seventies.

Soon after I had my own children, I joined the Oswestry Townswomen's Guild, but now I have been a member of Maesbury Women's Institute since 1998. My mother held lots of positions in the Townswomen's Guild and when I joined, they called my friends and me "the young ones", but now we are the older ones.

It was my friend Mary who invited me to join her at Maesbury WI as a friend she worked with was already a member. I love it as it is a very friendly organisation. There are some talented members at Maesbury, but members can participate in as much or as little as wished. We meet monthly and have a variety of speakers. We also enjoy various outings. On one occasion I won a bursary which enabled me to attend a course at the WI College in Oxford, called Denman. I took part in an Inspector Morse weekend which involved visiting numerous colleges and universities that were involved in the TV programme. I had my own en-suite room and the food was excellent.

Hospitals and Operations

I was a blood donor for around fifteen years, but recently retired. I hated needles when I was young, but now I don't mind needles at all. It's the same with operations. I spent many a restless night worrying about my hip operation, but to be honest, it wasn't scary at all and has definitely been worth it.

In 2012, I was expecting to be called to have a hip replacement operation in the February as I had been suffering for a long time, and it was gradually getting worse.

For a number of years, I had a stiff knee, but when seeing a consultant at the Orthopaedic Hospital he informed me the trouble was caused by arthritis in both hips. X-rays showed that the hips were worn out.

The final crunch came when staying in our caravan one summer holiday. I took the dogs out late one evening and I could hardly bear the pain. It was just too difficult to walk.

After visiting my GP, she asked me if I wanted to be put on the list for a hip replacement and after some hesitation, I agreed. When I hadn't heard anything by January, I rang the hospital to find out where I was on the waiting list. To my shock, I discovered they had received the letter from my GP, but no one had put my name on Mr. Graham's operating list. The earliest he could do the operation was May. I asked to be considered for a cancellation if any came up and one came up in April.

The day arrived, and I was extremely nervous when I checked in at seven o'clock in the morning having eaten nothing since the evening before. I was taken to the ward, hoping I wouldn't have long to wait. I was even hungrier when all the lunches began arriving. However, eventually a nurse arrived at about one in the afternoon.

"I'm sorry Mrs. Humby, but the previous patient is still in the theatre and her operation is taking longer than expected. We'll have to cancel your operation."

I was so disappointed but had no option but to ring Pat, who was waiting for news of a successful operation, asking him to collect me. I then had the task of telling people that it had been cancelled.

The next morning, I rang the hospital, "Can you confirm that my original date in May still stands?"

She went, but came back a moment later to inform me, "I'm sorry, this has now been given to someone else and you will have to wait until June."I was absolutely gutted.

Finally on 13th June 2012, I again checked in at seven o'clock in the morning. There were four ladies in the ward, all waiting to have hip replacements. We became friendly, but they were all at least twenty years younger than me. Luckily, this time I didn't wait too long and was soon wheeled up to theatre. By this time, I was desperate to for it to be over.

As I entered the theatre there were beds and trolleys everywhere and a nurse bent over me and said, "Oh, its Mavis, isn't it? I used to be a nurse at your vet's."

Eventually, they found me an empty bay and wrapped a lovely warm blanket around me. I was then wheeled in a chair to the anaesthetic room. My surgeon, Mr. Graham appeared, and I was soon asleep. After what seemed like a short while, someone was talking to me and asking if I was okay, then told me the operation was all over.

I was rather annoyed at being awakened as I was in the middle of a lovely dream, but also felt very relieved. Back in the ward, I enjoyed a sandwich and a cup of tea. That evening Pat was surprised at how chatty I was. The downside was while I had no pain at all in my hip, I suffered awful knee pain. The surgeon must have twisted it while replacing my hip.

The physiotherapist arrived the next morning to get me out of bed. They gave me a frame, and I began to walk, but the next thing I remember is seeing a pattern in front of my eyes and everything turned black. When I awoke I was flat on the floor with several faces peering down at me.

My blood pressure had dropped and I had fainted. I couldn't believe it as I had never fainted in my life. My operation was certainly not as frightening as I had feared, and I was even able to give myself anti-clotting injections daily for a month. I didn't have any stitches that had to be removed as they were dissolvable. I recovered well and was discharged after only three days. I had no pain in that hip, but the other was still very painful. The worst thing of all was I had to sleep on my back for six weeks.

Pat visited the day of my operation and again the following day, but that evening in the middle of the night he woke not feeling well with his heart beating irregularly. He phoned Lisa as he was alone in the house and she immediately drove over and rang 999. An ambulance arrived and Pat was taken to the Accident and Emergency department at the Royal Shrewsbury Hospital.

They decided not to tell me and as the Sunday was Father's day, Nick visited his dad in Shrewsbury and then came to see me in the Orthopaedic hospital in Oswestry with Lisa, who was also in charge of our three dogs. They told me about Pat and I was then discharged that afternoon, but Pat was kept in hospital for a further 24 hours.

Lisa was fantastic, waiting on me hand and foot, as well as seeing to the dogs and it was nice to spend time with her.

In July that year, a month after I came out of hospital Pat and I discussed whether to carry on touring with our large caravan, or whether it was time to purchase a static holiday home. We looked on the Internet, and then visited Salop Leisure in Shrewsbury. The first holiday home they showed us was a bit too old. The second one was perfect, but the question was where would we have it sited? The salesman looked on his computer and showed us three sites that would suit our needs. After receiving a reasonable offer for our tourer, we bought it. A few days later we had a day out in mid and North Wales to view the sites offered.

The first park we visited, known as Morben Isaf, was perfect, and we both loved it. It was three miles out of Machynlleth on the Aberystwyth road, which meant we could be there in just over the hour. It was thirty minutes from Aberystwyth, twenty minutes from Aberdovey, and thirty minutes from Towyn. There are beautiful beaches in all directions. We loved the first site which had lovely views, but we still visited the other two. These sites were not as nice. We rang Salop Leisure to confirm which holiday park we liked. We were so excited and could not wait to have the caravan sited. This happened on Pat's birthday, 30th July 2012, and we went to stay in our new holiday home two weeks later.

We certainly made the right decision and love visiting this gorgeous spot, which is usually every other week. The sun always seems to be shining and an added bonus is that we are right next to the Dyfi Osprey Centre. The ospreys return each spring from Senegal to the Cors Dyfi Centre to breed and they often fly over our caravan park. Towards the end of August, the female returns to Africa followed a few weeks later by her chicks, and finally the male. It is amazing how the ospreys find their way.

The following November, just five months after my first hip replacement, I went into the Orthopaedic to have my right one replaced. This time with no emergencies!

I had arranged for Lisa to stay at our house while I was in hospital. I cannot fault either of my times in the Orthopaedic, because it was like a first-class hotel and the food was lovely. I once again signed in at seven o'clock in the morning, and also met the same nurse in the preparation room as on the first occasion.

"This is the lady who fostered lots of children," she told the doctor. I felt like saying, "Get on with it, please!" That is the last thing I recall as the next moment I was back on the ward.

That evening all I wanted to do was sleep, but the lady in the bed opposite snored the loudest I have ever heard. I wanted to throw something heavy at her as it took me ages to go to sleep. I recovered even quicker this time and could walk around the bed on the second day. I was out of pain and didn't even faint this time. After three weeks, I did not need my crutches.

Each morning patients were able to choose the meals for the following day. The nurses were extremely busy, but they answered my every need at the press of a button. I would recommend anyone who is suffering to go ahead and have the operation.

The next thing I would need is a new knee as this was damaged as a result of my bad hips. I am so lucky to live near such a wonderful hospital. I could not believe how many phone and text messages I received after both operations, and the house resembled a florist's shop. I would have thought I had open heart surgery at the sheer amount of love I received! My good friend Mary even arrived with several meals she had cooked.

In late 2014 my left knee began to trouble me. I had left it too long before taking action and walked in a certain way to compensate for my painful hips, so the left knee became permanently bent. Reluctantly I consulted my doctor who referred me to the surgeon who had operated on both my hips and after a while I received an appointment. When he looked at the X-ray he said I had arthritis in both knees, the left being worse than the right. He put me on the waiting list and some months later I received a date in February 2015.

The operation went well, although painful and I had to attend physiotherapy for some weeks.

Unfortunately, the wound had an infection, and I had to have strong antibiotics, which made me feel poorly. After having the dressings changed many times, it eventually healed, but my leg was still bent, although not as much as before the operation.

When I went for my six-monthly check-up with Mr. Graham, he offered to attempt to straighten it more.

"There is a risk I could break your leg, although it hasn't happened to me yet," he told me.

By then, I could not cope with any more pain and opted to try the exercises instead.

I had been hoping my right knee would not need attention for some years, but unfortunately in early 2016 it began to hurt until I had no option but to ask my doctor to refer me back to my surgeon.

I felt depressed and anxious about it and on one occasion Mr. Graham's assistant asked, "What would you like to happen Mrs. Humby?"

"I want the pain to go away without another operation." I was already having trouble sleeping due to worrying.

He smiled, "Unfortunately, we can't do that, so it's an operation or take painkillers for the rest of your life."

I didn't want to be relying on tablets to get me through the days and nights, so I decided to be brave and had my second knee replaced at the end of November 2016. I also decided against having a general anaesthetic, opting for sedation instead, as the recovery time is quicker. I was worried as I didn't want to see or hear anything, but was assured that I wouldn't.

Things had changed for the better at the hospital since the last time and I was put in a private bay right from the beginning of the check-in process. The anaesthetist remembered me from my previous operation.

The sedation drug must have been strong, as I didn't remember a thing after entering the prep room. Mr. Graham was suddenly standing at the end of the bed asking if I was ok.

"I feel wonderful," I told him, hardly believing it was over.

"You may suffer some pain later" he said and he was not wrong. The second night I was in agony and kept asking for stronger medication. Things did improve and this time I didn't get an infection.

Three days later I was discharged on crutches. On the first morning after leaving the hospital, Pat wanted me to accompany him to choose a new dining room light fitting. I hobbled into the shop, pointed to the one I wanted and hobbled straight back to the car.

Pat did a wonderful job in caring for me. He cooked beautiful meals, looked after both dogs and cleaned the house, all while I had my feet up.

Lisa, my daughter, is a volunteer dog walker for the Cinnamon Trust, a charity which helps people care for their dogs if they become unable to do so themselves. Before my operation, Lisa had been walking a beautiful black standard poodle for an elderly lady in her nineties. Lisa often called in to see me and brought the poodle with her. Clicquot is beautiful, and a very regal looking dog. Having seen the standard poodles some years before when we visited Crufts, I fell in love with them but didn't think I would ever be able to afford one. Clicquot's owner then fell ill and was admitted to hospital, so Lisa offered to have the dog at her house until she recovered.

It soon became apparent the lady wouldn't be able to have her back and then decisions had to be made when the lady died. Lisa was already staying at our house as I was still in hospital. The day I returned was the day we became official owners of a standard poodle!

It certainly wasn't planned, but we do not regret it as we love her. She is so ladylike and has a lovely nature. She isn't very fond of our Chihuahua, but tolerates her. As we lost our gorgeous German Shepherd Indy suddenly in 2015 at the age of seven, it filled the gap for Pat.

Although it was me who initially wanted her, it is Pat whom she worships.

For several years we travelled twice a year by coach to London, organised by our friend John and his wife Ann, to see different musicals. It took so much organising as we had to arrange for children and dogs to be cared for, but it was worth it. We have seen scores of lovely musicals. Unfortunately, we had to stop because I found walking far too difficult, and even though I have now all four joints replaced, we haven't pursued it again.

In April 2013, my hairdresser told me I should get a small spot on my temple checked, and while my doctor was looking at that I asked him to look at a flaky patch on my left shoulder. He arranged for me to see a dermatologist. The appointment was on a day we were going to our holiday home. As it was a boiling hot day, I told Pat to stay in the car with the dogs, as I shouldn't be too long.

To my horror as I entered the consulting room at the Royal Shrewsbury Hospital the nurse shook my hand and introduced herself as the Macmillan Cancer nurse. I nearly passed out with shock. They called in the doctor to explain the area on my shoulder was a Basil Cell Carcinoma and would have to be removed. The doctors took a biopsy from the spot on my temple and informed me it was the most common type of skin cancer and would not spread to other areas. However, I was not convinced and walked out in a daze to tell Pat. I had a very worried journey to our caravan in Machynlleth.

I returned to the hospital in June 2013 for the removal operation and must say that the whole procedure was painless. I feel blessed that I was able to endure these operations, and that I had my family's support throughout each ordeal.

Our Final Placement

One of the places we loved to visit with our tourer was Sandringham Caravan Park. There are miles of beautiful woodland to walk in and often deer roam there. In May 2011, we were preparing to spend a week there when we received a request to foster another newborn, who had been born ten weeks before his due date. He was in the Royal Shrewsbury Maternity Unit. When Social Services approached us, they hadn't yet received the necessary authority to move the baby, but as we were going away, he would go to a temporary carer until we returned.

He weighed just over two pounds when he was born, but now was a bit more than four. We couldn't believe how small he was. When we returned he was still in the hospital, so he hadn't needed to go to the other carer. We arranged the time and day to arrive and collect him, and went to the premature baby unit. He was so tiny and absolutely perfect. He was the smallest baby ever in our care.

The nurse showed us how to give him his special formula and then we had to meet and discuss all his medical needs with another staff member. It was all quite scary, especially as we watched a video on resuscitation.

Some three hours later we lifted him into the car seat where he looked even smaller, and returned home. As soon as I arrived home with him I became more confident. He was such a dear little chap who was in care because his mother was homeless and she had already had four other children removed. This was her fifth child with three different fathers. One of them had moved to an adoptive placement, one was living with his paternal grandparents, and two were in long-term foster care. The father of the baby was a drug addict.

We met the baby's mother and got on well with her. Initially she had daily contact as she said she was breastfeeding, but it turned out this wasn't true.

Every week he gained weight, and we received our first smile not much later than if he had been a full-term baby. Each morning we received visits from a member of the medical staff from the hospital premature unit, but over a period this stopped. Everywhere we went he received so much attention. He resembled a little Barbie doll. We just loved him! Nobody could believe how tiny he was, but so perfect. Little did we realise then that he would be our last placement.

Unfortunately, while we were staying at my son's house in Kent one weekend in August 2011, the baby became very unsettled. He was four months old. I knew instinctively something wasn't right. I consulted my daughter-in-law who was a staff nurse at the hospital in Ashford, and we agreed we should take him to outpatients to be checked.

At the time she was preparing a chicken dinner, but I didn't want to delay things, so we dropped everything and off we went. Owing to the fact that he was so young and small, we didn't have to wait long to see a doctor. He examined him and informed us he needed an operation that day for a hernia.

Apparently, this can often happen in premature babies, particularly boys. They said an ambulance would take the baby and me to St. Thomas' Hospital in London, which is situated right near the Houses of Parliament. Before he began this journey, they had to insert a cannula into his leg to keep him hydrated during the journey. Pat then took our daughter-in-law and her children back home.

The procedure proved quite difficult as he was so small and it wasn't pleasant watching blood spurt over the white sheet as he screamed in discomfort. However, after what seemed like an eternity we boarded the ambulance accompanied by a very friendly ambulance assistant. These ambulances are not built for comfort, and with blue lights flashing we began the bumpy ride. It was around ten o'clock at night when we arrived at the hospital, which was very busy with many children and their parents. All of them waiting to be seen. I sat with the baby in a small side room and after a while a doctor examined him and informed me that they wouldn't be operating until the next day, so I could give him his bottle. A nurse promised me a cup of tea, but this didn't arrive until one and a half hours later.

Now there were two extremely lucky things that happened. One was I had only recently obtained the baby's birth mother's mobile number, so I could inform her of the situation. I knew I would need her permission for him to have the operation. She agreed. The other was, very unusually, I had the baby's social worker's home number, and I rang for advice.

My next worry was I had no way of charging my mobile, and with letting Pat know what was happening it was rapidly running low on battery. I still had a number of calls to make. Luckily it did last until the mother of the baby in the next bed lent me her charger and I was able to phone Pat to bring me in some essentials, including a box of cereal. The social worker rang her superior, and he informed me of what had to be done before the baby's operation.

At around eleven o'clock the hospital told me we would soon be admitted to a ward. It was nearly midnight when I was finally led down a long corridor from the old part of the hospital to the new posh part. It was quite a walk, crossing on a walkway over a busy street and travelling up in two glass lifts. Finally, we reached a ward with dimmed lights where everyone was asleep. I thought I would have to sleep in a chair but no, the father of a baby opposite me showed me how to pull out a bed that dropped down from the wall.

I had no comb, make-up or night wear, or any washing things and just lay down fully clothed. The nurse made a lovely nest out of blankets for the baby.

I was told the baby couldn't be fed after six o'clock in the morning as the surgery was planned for the next day, although they didn't know what time. I didn't sleep well knowing I would have to feed him at five o'clock in the morning, but it was better than sleeping in a chair.

Next morning I was told the canteen didn't open over the weekend and apart from drinks, I would have to leave the hospital and walk to a nearby shopping centre to buy something to eat. They only feed the patients, not the parents.

Although my little boy needed another bottle, all I was allowed to give him was water. He became agitated, so a male nurse agreed to look after him while I went to find myself something to eat. It seemed like miles until I reached a shop which involved walking down lots of corridors and travelling down two lifts. I was able to buy a sandwich and some fruit.

A manager from Social Services then rang to say they gave permission for the baby to have whatever treatment was necessary, but the hospital insisted on speaking to his mother. I tried ringing her and leaving numerous messages on both hers and her mother's phone asking her to ring me or the hospital. It was some hours later when a doctor finally managed to speak to her and obtained the necessary permission. It was so stressful!

Pat arrived after lunch and had difficulty finding the hospital as this was following the awful riots in London. Finally, at around five o'clock at night, Pat and I accompanied the baby as he was pushed in his cot down two floors to the operating theatre. We both felt emotional to see this tiny little boy being given an anesthetic. We returned to the ward to wait for news that he was ready to return.

After over an hour we went to recovery where four nurses were cooing over him. He was still only eight pounds in weight. A porter pushed him back to the ward, and I was now able to give him a feed.

That evening I pulled my bed down early as I was so tired. I woke once to feed the baby, but otherwise slept like a log. The first thing I was

112

aware of was a doctor standing by the bed talking to me. With uncombed hair and wearing no makeup, I must have looked an awful sight.

"The baby can go home today, Mrs Humby and as you live so far away, you can take him to your local hospital for his post-operative check-up."

It was nice to hear we wouldn't have to return to St. Thomas', although the treatment was nothing but the best. I managed to message Pat asking him to come and collect us.

We travelled back to Nick's home in Ashford on the Sunday morning, but soon after decided we had better go home a day sooner than we had originally planned. Soon after our return, the scar was hardly visible and since then he has no recurrence of the problem. I shall certainly remember my visit to London!

When this little boy was nine months old, the decision was made that he should be placed for adoption as his mother's situation hadn't improved. A couple in their twenties were chosen and an Information Meeting arranged.

I felt anxious about meeting this couple, dearly hoping they would be suitable for this gorgeous little boy. I walked into the side room where they were nervously waiting and couldn't help myself.

"Do you realise you are having a beautiful little boy?"

I instantly took to them as they admitted how nervous they were and realised their lives would never be the same again.

After chatting for a short while we then went into the meeting. They weren't allowed to meet the baby yet and didn't know he was outside with Pat in the car. The introduction plan was arranged and the first meeting happened two days later at our house.

Gradually the visits increased in length. At the end of the week, we would all meet up with Social Services to see if the adoption would go ahead. During that time, they took him for walks, fed him, played with him and even put him to bed after his bath. The last thing that took place was us visiting his new home and we were so impressed at how prepared they were.

At the final meeting all went well and they certainly hadn't changed their minds. We reported back to Social Services saying the contacts had all gone well, so the day was fixed when they would come to take him home permanently with them. We were completely in agreement that he would have a wonderful home with lovely parents.

The first evening he was with them they rang to say he had gone to bed okay, which was nice to hear. They kept us informed of his progress over the following months and invited us to the court when the final adoption was confirmed. They finally had a son and we were so happy that everything had gone so well.

They have visited us at our holiday home and came to see me in the hospital after my first hip replacement operation. They are so proud of him and he seemed to have reached all his milestones. He doesn't remember us, but we will never forget him. What a lucky couple to have such a darling, and what a lucky little boy to have found a lovely family!

It is so rewarding to follow the progress of the past children in our care. When a child moves on it sometimes feels like a bereavement. Previously I mentioned how we were at the christening of a little girl and I felt sad she no longer belonged to us. As time goes on I have learned to take a backseat when really all I want to do is to scoop them up in my arms and run.

When this last little boy moved in the January, I was waiting for my hip replacement in February. We were to be given twelve months off from fostering and any longer meant we would have to go through training again.

Retirement

The following January we had to make a decision as to whether we wanted to return to fostering. The twelve months sabbatical Social Services had given us was coming to an end. To return after one year would mean retraining as if we were new carers. We gave this much thought and decided, as we had finished with the perfect placement, maybe it was time to call it a day. It was a hard decision, but I think the right one as we were now in our seventies.

We wrote our letter of resignation and sent it. The following day it came to my knowledge that a carer friend from Oswestry was waiting for a new baby to arrive and I was very tempted to say we had changed our minds as I felt very jealous. However, the feeling passed.

On 7th September 2013, we spent a wonderful weekend celebrating our golden wedding anniversary. We visited Oswald Road Church where we had married fifty years before in the rain. At least it was sunny for our anniversary! It is now an antique centre and we took a picture on the same steps where we had been photographed fifty years earlier.

We also had a photograph taken with our friends Joyce and Tony Cawkwell, who had been married in Yorkshire on the same day. The photo was published in the Oswestry Advertizer. We have celebrated our wedding anniversaries with them for many years. They organised a party at Oswestry Golf Club on the Saturday evening of which many of our mutual friends attended. On the Sunday morning, at my request, our children and grandchildren attended the morning service at our church, after which we all enjoyed lunch at the Sweeney Hall Hotel.

We have had a few ups and downs over the last fifty-five years, but feel proud that we are still together. I have had a happy and fulfilling life, and although I never thought I would say it, I am now enjoying my retirement. I can concentrate on my children, grandchildren and foster grandchildren and spend more time with Pat and our friends.

The best thing Pat and I ever did was to purchase a holiday home at Morben Isaf, to escape the everyday life. I enjoy good health and hope we can enjoy many more years of retirement and happy marriage.

Before this story is finalised, I must mention my birth grandchildren and foster grandchildren.

Adam and his partner Heidi have a son Levi and a daughter Lowrie.

Julie is mum to Hannah and Rosie.

Emma has a son, Richard

Jenny has an older daughter, Jess, two sons Tony and Oliver, and a baby girl, Amber.

Jenny is also a grandmother as Jess and Ashley are parents to Leo, Emily, Mikey and Ruby, with another on the way.

I am so proud of them all, as they are wonderful parents.

Last, but not least, are my birth grandchildren. Nick and Cher have a daughter Stacey and a son Mathew. Stacey has certainly inherited a love of animals, and I am extremely proud of them all.

Mavis Humby

116

I hope you enjoyed this book and I'd really appreciate it if you would post a short review on Amazon. I read all the reviews personally.

Thanks for your support.

Printed in Great Britain
by Amazon

77933837R00068